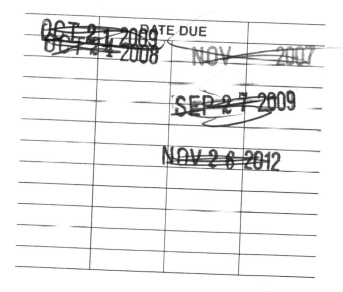

Learning About

FALL

with Children's Literature

Learning About
FALL
with Children's Literature

Cross-curricular units based on the works of Eric Carle, Robert Kalan, Ludwig Bemelmans, and more

Margaret A. Bryant, Marjorie Keiper, and Anne Petit

Zephyr Press

Chicago

Cover design: Monica Baziuk

© 2006 by Margaret A. Bryant, Marjorie Keiper, and Anne Petit
All rights reserved
Published by Zephyr Press
An imprint of Chicago Review Press, Incorporated
814 North Franklin Street
Chicago, Illinois 60610
ISBN-10: 1-56976-204-X
ISBN-13: 978-1-56976-204-2
Printed in the United States of America

DEDICATION

To Keith, Glenn, and Jim—
without your support this book could not have been written
and
to the First Graders of Old Trail School
—past, present, and future—
you were our inspiration

CONTENTS

INTRODUCTION

About the Program

The early primary classroom presents many challenges to the teacher who must provide an environment that nurtures strengths, addresses needs, develops strong academic skills, and encourages a positive self-concept. Students may be knowledgeable about many things but may lack some basic experiences that are necessary for success in an academic setting. A whole language approach can build a foundation that gives all students an opportunity to succeed.

We define whole language as a holistic approach to the teaching of reading and writing. A whole language approach employs seeing, hearing, reading, and writing words to develop the competencies children need to become fluent, independent readers and writers. Phonetic skills, the foundation of a comprehensive literacy program, are presented during the daily poetry session.

Trade books offer the opportunity to learn to read through stories that are interesting, support in-depth and varied questioning, and encourage a love of literature in young children. These books establish a common ground that allows students who have had limited experience with books to interact with more privileged peers. The content also provides a basis for higher-level questioning and enrichment activities that will challenge more capable students.

We are aware of the wide range of abilities found in most early primary classrooms. At the age some children are independent learners while others are still struggling to grasp basic skills and need many opportunities for reinforcement. It takes a magician to create a warm, nurturing environment in which children with such differing needs will be successful. This book offers ideas for the child who is an emerging reader as well as for those children who are reading far above their grade level. The common books and themes of this program give all students the opportunity to interact successfully while being challenged at the appropriate instructional level. Because children of varying abilities use the same material, although in different ways, emerging readers do not feel that they are in a different reading group.

The whole language approach encourages children to view writing as positively as they view reading. Inability to spell a word does not prevent a child from using it. The child simply writes the sounds he or she hears or, early on, the first letter, and draws a line for the remainder of the word. Confidence, competency, and fluency develop rapidly in this accepting atmosphere.

Thematic units incorporate other subjects into the reading program. As teachers are being asked to include more and more in the curriculum, this method of organization allows maximum use of the school day. The broad range of available trade books makes it easy to meet science or social studies objectives while children are receiving reading instruction.

A limited budget may be a factor in establishing a program that relies on trade books. Although it is ideal to have many copies of the books when implementing this program, other options exist. One rather time-consuming possibility is to get many copies from school and community libraries. If only one copy is available, you can read the story to the class, have the children choose eighteen to twenty words from that story for instructional purposes, and then have children rewrite the story in their own words. You can then copy this story on chart paper, the chalkboard, or individual sheets for students to use during instructional reading time.

One advantage of the latter method is that the children identify with the story and have a sense of ownership, which can be powerful tool for young readers because what they write they are also able to read. For example, if you are using *If You Give a Mouse a Cookie*, students may choose *refrigerator* as one of the focal words. Though this word is not typically considered a first-grade word, it has high interest value, and less exciting (but just as useful) words must be employed to create a sentence. Thus *refrigerator* becomes the tool to help children learn words such as *the* and *that*.

Structure of Plans

Lesson plans are keyed with the following symbols:

EL (emerging learners): Children who are working below grade level or need extra support

TL (typical learners): Students who are performing at grade level

AL (advanced learners): Children whose abilities require more challenging activities

Whole language is a successful method for teaching young children to read, write, and spell, but because it is less structured than a basal program, some teachers are reluctant to use it. This book offers a way to support all the skills necessary for creating a strong literacy foundation for young children. Although you can introduce skills in a variety of ways, we have made suggestions for presenting skills on a weekly basis. In this program, all basic skills are introduced, reinforced, and assessed.

We suggest group instruction for introducing a reading selection, but you will also have many opportunities for small-group and individual instruction. You will need to group children as their needs dictate for reteaching or remedial work. Typically, some students will understand and master skills the first time they are presented, whereas other children will need several sessions. You will have to determine what is best for the children in your classroom.

Poetry and Skills

Poems are an obvious vehicle for teaching rhyming words, but they are equally effective for learning vowels, blends, and contractions, as well as other skills necessary for a child to become a strong, independent reader. In the program described here, the skills lessons are presented to the whole class during shared reading of the daily poem.

We have selected poems to coordinate with the thematic units. In our program, children memorize one poem each month. During the first week of the month, you will introduce the poem, discuss it, and display it in a prominent place. You will give each child a copy to illustrate and place in an individual poetry notebook and another to take home to memorize. When a child recites the poem, place a sticker on that page in the notebook. You might also write the child's name on a seasonal cut-out and attach it to the displayed poem. In our classrooms we have cut-outs that coordinate with the monthly theme. There is no award given to the first child who recites the poem nor any particular notice to the child who is last. The public record is merely a reminder to those who have not learned the poem, and it offers the teacher a quick check on the progress of the class.

How to Get Started

Educators often assume that children who are reading independently do not need the same skills lessons as typical readers or those who read below grade level. This assumption is a grave error. Although some children may read early, they may not know important labels or have decoding strategies, which can cause them problems later on. A child may be able to read "isn't," for example, but might not understand contractions. These students need to build the same foundation as their classmates, although they may be able to do so at a quicker pace.

Grouping

Our philosophy is that the daily lessons should be presented in whole group sessions, but we also recognize that children learn at different rates and have different needs. We have therefore organized the lessons so that the objective is introduced to the class as a whole, but direct instruction is handled in smaller groups.

Children will be placed in various groups for various instructional purposes. For example, after you introduce a new book you might place the students into small groups that have a mix of ability levels. Children will read the story orally, which allows the more capable students to support the emerging readers. In another session, children who need extra help with a particular decoding skill will meet in a small group for reinforcement. Although children will recognize the more fluent readers, when they are grouped for purposes other than ability, no one feels like a "crow" instead of a "bluebird." The sensitive teacher keeps groups fluid so children are comfortable with and have opportunities to interact with all their classmates.

Author of the Month

Each month an author is featured and several of his or her books are included in the reading plans. The students learn about the author's childhood, other careers he or she pursued, the author's struggle for perfection, and some of the obstacles that had to be overcome before the author gained recognition for his or her work. This material will help young readers gain an understanding of the person who wrote, and in many cases illustrated, the books.

Other children enjoy writing to authors, many of whom are sensitive to their young audiences and will respond to fan letters. Letters from authors should be kept in a scrapbook for the class, parents, and other interested parties to read. At the end of the year each letter should become the property of the child who received the letter. You can find addresses for authors at the reference desk of your local library or through the publisher.

Thematic Structure

This program employs a thematic approach that incorporates other subject areas into the reading program. Each month there is an academic focus around which the language arts block is organized.

Using Music

Music is an important part of all curriculum plans. Children are naturally expressive and should be encouraged to explore this expressiveness through musical experiences. The elements of rhythm, form, melody, and harmony contribute to the emotional quality of music. We intend the selections in this program to enhance children's appreciation for music. It will help young children appreciate and interpret musical messages if they have a basic understanding of the language of music. You can adapt the open-ended activities that follow for use with any musical selection chosen for the primary classroom.

Comparisons

To develop an awareness of the different means of expression used in music, select two different pieces, such as lullaby and a march. Play a recording of the lullaby and ask the children to verbalize how the music makes them feel. Play the march and ask them the same question. Encourage children to compare and contrast the two pieces. Your students could also move rhythmically to the music to feel how two different dances require the same or different body movements.

Scribble drawings

You can encourage students to express themselves to music through scribble drawings and tone paintings. For scribble drawings, ask students to make uninterrupted scribble designs with crayons on paper while listening to a musical selection. Later they can attempt to create from their scribbles forms that the music suggested.

Tone paintings

After listening to one (or more) pieces, children might paint their own interpretations while listening to the music.

Journals

Tempo and dynamics set many different moods. Help children learn to identify the various musical instruments and verbalize the feelings the instruments create after listening to a specific piece. Students could keep musical journals to record their thoughts on selections they have listened to and enjoyed. They might include musical illustrations in their journals.

Symbols and vocabulary

To help children understand the symbols and terms used to represent expression in music, cut tag board into strips—or use commercially prepared sentence strips—and on each strip write one of the following symbols or terms:

<	crescendo	gradually louder
>	decrescendo	gradually softer
f	forte	loud
ff	fortissimo	very loud
mf	mezzo forte	medium loud
mp	mezzo piano	medium soft
p	piano	soft
pp	pianissimo	very soft
	allegro	fast
	andante	slow
	moderato	moderately

Use the cards to make a game of matching terms and symbols. Or you might try passing out the cards to the children and asking questions such as, *If you have a card that means to play or sing very loudly, hold up your card.* You can also use the cards while you are listening to various selections. Have children hold up an appropriate card to describe what they hear happening in the music. They might be surprised to see how quickly the cards change and how often each one is used throughout the selection.

Scope and Sequence

This section offers an overview of each month's objectives. Our goal has been to organize the material in a flexible manner that will allow teachers to incorporate it into their individual curricula. Activities for science, social studies, math, music, art, and French are included in the weekly lessons, but not all subjects are included in each unit. Although the only foreign language we have included is French, many materials in other languages are available and can be substituted in accordance with the mandates of individual curricula.

SEPTEMBER

Author: Eric Carle

English Skills
    Phonetic Skills
    Vowels
        Short and long e
            Short and long o
        Rhyming Words
    Structural analysis
        Nouns
        Verbs
    Punctuation
        Capital Letters
        Periods
    Comprehension
        Alphabetical sequence
    Prediction
        Word families
        Sequence of events
        Number words

Science Skills
    Classifying insects
    Metamorphosis
    Life cycle of insects
    Comparing insects and spiders
    Migration of some insects
Math Skills
    Calendar
    Graphing
    Symmetry
    Counting sets
    Days of the week

OCTOBER

Author: Bill Martin, Jr.

English Skills
Phonetic Skills
Short and long e, u
Vowel followed by r
ow and ou
Structural analysis
Adjectives
Nouns and verbs
Root words and endings
Compound words
Comprehension
Sequence
Cause and effect
Main idea
Punctuation
Question marks
Capital letters
Periods
Quotation marks

Science Skills
Life cycle of a frog
Seeds
Plants
Leaves
Seasonal changes
Math Skills
Graphing
Measuring
Problem solving
Story problems
Social Studies
Christopher Columbus
Map skills

NOVEMBER

Author: Ludwig Bemelmans

English Skills
Phonetic Skills
Vowels
Short and long a, i
Word families
Rule of silent e
Structural analysis
Adjectives
Rhyming words
Compounds
Alphabetizing to the first letter
Comprehension
Cause and effect
Prediction

Social Studies Skills
France
Map skills
Purpose
Use
Location of cities
Pilgrims
Math Skills
Sequencing
Concept of a dozen
Foreign Language Skills
Landmarks in Paris
Comparing common French and
English terms

1
SEPTEMBER

Theme: Insects

Week 1: Overview

Instructional Book

The Very Hungry Caterpillar by Eric Carle

Related Titles

Animals, Animals by Eric Carle (to be read aloud)
Dragons, Dragons by Eric Carle (to be read aloud)
Other Eric Carle titles
I Wish I Were a Butterfly by James Howe (to be read aloud)

Poems

"Bug in a Jug" anonymous
"Keep a Poem in Your Pocket" by Beatrice de Regniers Schenk
"Oh the Toe-Test" by Norma Farber

Music

Papillons by Robert Schumann

Video

Eric Carle: Picture Writer. Directed by Rawn Fulton

Objectives

1. **Phonetic skills**
   Begin to understand short and long o.
2. **Structural analysis**
   Identify nouns.
   Recognize and build word families.
3. **Comprehension**
   Begin to make predictions.
   Begin to understand the sequence of events in a story.
   Recognize number words one through seven.

Materials

Word cards:
18 to 20 circles of green construction paper, approximately six inches in diameter, and one red circle that looks like the caterpillar's head. Write the vocabulary words on the green circles, laminate the cards, and, for magnets, attach pieces of magnetic tape to the backs.

Cards with the pictures of the food in *The Very Hungry Caterpillar*

Cards with the days of the week, number words one to seven, and the words *juicy, leaf, cocoon,* and *beautiful butterfly*

Self-stick removable note pads

Poetry and Skills Session

Strategies for Presenting Phonetic Skills

Before each poetry and skills session write the poem on a large sheet of chart paper. Laminate the poem so the children will be able to write on it with washable pens. The surface can be cleaned at the end of each session and the poems used over and over again.

Finding a way to store these poems certainly presents a challenge. We organize the poems by theme and month, clip them together with clothespins, and lay them flat in a storage closet. The clothespins are labeled with the name of the month, or theme, and the packages can be located easily.

As you introduce phonetic skills, the class records words that have related sounds. Students can add to these lists indefinitely and you can display them in several ways:

- Attach large chart paper to a wall in the classroom.

- Cover large empty boxes in paper and stack them in a corner with two of the sides displayed. Students will write a long vowel on one face and the short vowel on the other.

- Divide a bulletin board into sections.

- Suspend charts from the ceiling.

Word families are an effective way to extend vocabulary and reinforce rhyming words. Begin with a base and change the beginning sound. Involve the students in this process. For example:

og
hog
dog
frog

These lists of words serve as clues of the sounds of the letters and are also helpful when the students are doing creative writing.

DAY 1

"Keep a Poem in Your Pocket"

Step 1: Discuss the content and meaning of the verses.

Step 2: Identify the rhyming words. Observe the repetition of the chorus.

Step 3: Introduce the sound of long o.

Step 4: Have the children listen as the poem is read. After you have read the poem, have students name words in which they heard the sound. As you read the poem, give auditory clues by slightly emphasizing the appropriate words.

Step 5: Have the students point to the words that contain the sound. If the poem has been laminated the students can circle words with a washable pen.

Step 6: Reread the poem together at the end of the session and give each student a copy to be illustrated and placed in his or her poetry book.

Teacher's Tip

The poetry notebooks are a good tool to help children learn organizational skills. Take a few moments to help the children learn to

open and close binders while protecting their fingers

number the pages, beginning by placing a "1" in the upper right-hand corner of the first poem

turn the poems in the book to the left side of the cover when adding poems

place new poems face up on the right side

close the rings

move all poems to the right

If the children form the habit of numbering the poems, turning all pages to the left of the book, and placing the new poem at the end, they will find it easier to locate a particular poem to read aloud.

DAY 2

"Keep a Poem in Your Pocket"

Step 1: Reread the poem and review the sounds discussed.

Step 2: Introduce the sound of short o. Use several examples, then ask the children to find words in the poem that have the short o sound.

Step 3: Review the long o and compare the sounds of the two.

Step 4: Reread the poem together.

DAY 3

"Oh the Toe-Test"

Step 1: Read the poem to the class.
Step 2: Allow the children time to enjoy the rhythm of the poem.
Step 3: Discuss the meaning of the poem.
Step 4: Locate words that contain an o.
Step 5: Read these words and ask children to identify the sound the vowel makes. If the poem is laminated, circle words using one color for long o and a different color for the short o.
Step 6: Reread the poem together and distribute copies for the poetry books.

DAY 4

"Oh the Toe-Test"

Step 1: Read the poem with the class and allow time for comments and discussion.
Step 2: Review the vowel sounds.
Step 3: Choose a word from the poem, change the beginning sound to make a word family. Help the children use several of these words in a sentence, creating a short, original poem.

DAY 5

"Bug in a Jug"

This poem is intended to be humorous. The children will like the rhythm of the words.

Step 1: Read the poem once to the children and then several times with them.
Step 2: Discuss the rhythm of the poem and note that there are *no* rhyming words.
Step 3: Talk about the meaning of the short lines. Perhaps the children will enjoy dramatizing the poem.
Step 4: Read the poem a final time for fun.
Step 5: Distribute copies for poetry notebooks.

Reading Instruction

DAY 1

Biographical Sketch of Eric Carle

Eric Carle was born in Syracuse, New York, on June 25, 1929. His parents were German immigrants. While he was in kindergarten, he painted on large pieces of paper with bright colors and he remembers feeling very happy (de Montreville and Crawford, 1978).

His family moved back to Germany when he was six years old. He was not happy in his new home because he missed his friends and did not like his new, much stricter school. During this time he thought a lot about bridges and wished there was one that would take him back to America. He would have taken his German grandmother with him if it had been possible (Kovacs and Preller 1991).

Mr. Carle returned to the United States in 1950 and began his career as an artist. He designed book covers and began illustrating books for beginning readers. He found that he really liked working on books for children and began writing some of his own. His first book was called *1, 2, 3, to the Zoo*. It won a prize for illustrations in Italy and Germany (de Montreville and Crawford 1978). Perhaps his recollection of kindergarten art was one of the reasons he chose the technique of collage to illustrate his books.

He has a studio in his home where he paints tissue paper in unique colors and textures. These brightly colored papers become the illustrations for his stories (Norby and Ryan 1988). Mr. Carle draws the picture on the paper, uses the sketch as the pattern, and then cuts the shape from the tissue paper he has previously prepared. In *The Very Hungry Caterpillar* he tells the story from the perspective of the caterpillar, so the illustrations are large. He overlaps pieces of the tissue paper, which adds shading to the picture. He incorporates white space in the illustrations to add a positive and negative dimension to his work.

Children have told him that there is a mistake in *The Very Hungry Caterpillar* but Mr. Carle feels that the word "cocoon" sounds better in the text than "chrysalis" (Kovacs and Preller 1991).

After reading the biography of Eric Carle aloud to your students, discuss his illustrations with the class. Young children usually respond to the simplicity of his work and are quick to note his repeated use of a sun with rays of light.

The Very Hungry Caterpillar

Shared Reading

> Step 1: Discuss the cover and title of *The Very Hungry Caterpillar*.
>
> Step 2: Have children make predictions about the content. Record these predictions.
>
> Step 3: Read the story together. Encourage group response where appropriate. Example: "He was still hungry."
>
> Step 4: Reread the predictions and discuss them with children. Accept all contributions in a positive manner. It is necessary to help students feel free to make suggestions, even when the students are unsure. Respond in a positive way to the answers that are less appropriate. It takes courage for a child to risk being wrong.

Small Group Instruction

The following discussion questions are presented to each group and you should adjust your expectations to the abilities of the children. Encourage advanced students to respond with in-depth answers, while accepting more abbreviated answers from the other children. However, it is appropriate to encourage all students to elaborate.

> Discussion questions for the three groups:
>
> - What was the sequence of the items eaten?
>
> - Was the caterpillar greedy? Explain
>
> - How did the caterpillar feel at the end of the week?
>
> - What parts of the story could really happen and what parts couldn't?
>
> - How does this story compare to the actual facts known about caterpillars?

EL: Read with the children as a choral reading. Pause on different pages and have individuals read to find specific information.

TL: If appropriate, allow this group to read the whole book independently. They may read it as a play, or choose their favorite page.

AL: Have students read the book independently.

DAY 2

The Very Hungry Caterpillar

Shared Reading

> Step 1: Use self-stick notes to block out previously chosen vocabulary. Give

the students word cards on which these words have been written. As the group reads the story, have the children supply the missing words.

Step 2: Identify "name words" (nouns). Begin a chart of insect nouns. Encourage children to add to the list daily. Students may begin a caterpillar dictionary in which they write the words, illustrate them, and perhaps use them in a sentence. At this early stage many young children have limited skills and endurance for writing assignments. Use activities that are appropriate to their developmental levels.

Small Group Instruction

EL: Have individuals choose a favorite page to read orally. Use word cards from the shared reading session for vocabulary development.

TL: Have children work in pairs and read to each other. Observe the fluency of the readers and note those who need assistance. Use cards from the shared reading session for vocabulary development.

AL: Oral reading is important for this group also. Allow them to read with partners, and informally evaluate fluency, expression and comprehension. Students choose the vocabulary words and make up new sentences. They could make up word riddles and have others in the group guess the word. This activity could be done with a mix of students from all groups.

DAY 3

The Very Hungry Caterpillar

Shared Reading

Step 1: Discuss illustrations. Compare them to those in other Eric Carle titles.

Step 2: Children play a sequence game with the food from the story. Students can use items on a flannel board to retell the story. They can match pictures to words.

Step 3: Have children discuss the picture of the butterfly at the end of the story. Is it a real butterfly? Encourage the students to use their knowledge of butterflies to support their answers.

Step 4: Read the story aloud and, before you turn each page, have someone place the picture of the next item the caterpillar eats, the corresponding word, and the appropriate number word on a chalk tray or other surface.

Small Group Instruction

All groups

Step 1: Combine groups in a mix of fluent and emergent readers. Have children read the story in pairs or trios.

Step 2: Encourage the children to discuss the story among themselves. What did they like about the story? Could this story be used with a different insect? What food was their favorite? Would they have added any other food?

DAY 4

Shared Reading

During this session read aloud a book about moths and butterflies. Have students compare the facts in this story to what happens in *The Very Hungry Caterpillar*. Record their responses on a chart. Label the statements "Fact" and "Fiction." Allow time for the students to discuss the two books.

Small Group Instruction

EL: Hold up individual vocabulary words from *The Very Hungry Caterpillar*. Have students locate and read aloud the sentences in which they appear. Allow volunteers to choose a word and use it in a sentence while you write the sentence on the board. Because children choose their own words, they naturally select those that they are able to read; this activity gives all a feeling of success. After each child has had a turn, ask the group to read the sentences together.

TL: This group follows the same procedure as the previous group. Allow the children to take turns placing the days in order and matching the other words to the appropriate day.

AL: This group will be able to perform the same activity but in less time. Encourage them to arrange the cards to show the day, the food, and so on. Suggest that they work together to create a story about "A Very Hungry _____ ." They can write the stories or tell them to the group. They will enjoy making puppets or using original cut-outs of the characters when telling their story.

DAY 5

Shared Reading

Read a new Eric Carle title to the class and compare the illustrations, the theme of the story, and the characters with those in *The Very Hungry Caterpillar*. How are the books alike, and how are they different? Allow students time to discuss Mr. Carle's artistic style and recall what they learned in the biographical sketch.

Small Group Instruction

Creative Writing

Place the vocabulary from *The Very Hungry Caterpillar* somewhere where children can see it. Distribute large sheets of paper to the children and have them fold the paper into fourths. In each box, each child will write a sentence using one of the vocabulary words and illustrate the sentence. When they are finished, have them cut the sections apart, staple them together, and make a cover for their books.

This activity gives children a foundation to begin creative writing. They will probably ask often for correct spellings of words. Suggest they tell what sounds they hear in the word and write those sounds down, stating that if they can read their stories, the spelling is good enough. They will need time to develop the confidence to use invented spelling and this process will be helpful.

Independent Activities

Materials Needed

Three lists of words: one with the days of the week, one with the foods named in the book, and one with numbers *one* through *seven*

Green construction paper and a circle pattern.

Newsprint, 12 by 18 inches

Beans, macaroni, curly pasta, and pasta bows

Pressed paper egg cartons

Pipe cleaners

Paper lunch sacks

Manila paper

Extension Activities

- At this stage students' writing skills are limited, so it is better to ask children to draw their ideas. Duplicate words and pictures from *The Very Hungry Caterpillar* and have children cut them apart, place them in sequence, and illustrate them.

- Have students illustrate the life cycle of a butterfly. Students will write words in boxes numbered 1 through 4 and illustrate each stage using beans for the egg, macaroni for the pupa, curly pasta for the chrysalis, and a pasta bow for the adult.

- Begin an insect book that students will add to throughout the unit. Draw a picture of a large insect on the board. Label the parts. Children each make their own drawing and write the names of the parts.

- Develop a caterpillar corner. Have the children paint sections of egg cartons, attach pipe cleaners for antenna, and draw or glue on eyes. These creations go in the caterpillar corner. Display a calendar in the corner and discuss the length of time it takes for a butterfly to emerge from a cocoon. Place the "caterpillar" in a paper sack "cocoon". Mark the days off the calendar. During the "metamorphic period," have students make butterflies. On the day the insects are to chrysalize, put the adults made by the students into the sacks. Have students take them out.

Construction of Butterfly

- Fold 12-by-18-inch sheets of manila paper in half. Have each child draw a large butterfly on one side of one sheet. Holding the paper carefully, cut the butterflies from both sheets so the student has two identical insects. They color a top and bottom. Spread paste on the blank side and fit both together. Then have students mold the butterfly over the side of the hand or a pencil. The wings can be turned up and they will hold their shape.

- Have children write their own version of *The Very Hungry Caterpillar*. For younger children, you may have them dictate their stories to you as you write them. Prepare small books for this purpose and have students illustrate the stories.

Small Group and Center Activities

- Copy the lists of the days of the week and the foods described in the materials so you have two lists for each student. Direct the children to cut apart the words, match the foods with the days, paste them on sheets of paper, and illustrate.

- Give the students copies of the number words one through seven. Have them cut the words apart, paste them on paper, and illustrate them.

- Write a selected vocabulary on the board. Using a pattern and green paper, have the students cut out circles, print one word on each circle and form their own caterpillars. They should take these with them and practice the words at home.

- Have the students fold a 12-by-18-inch sheet of paper three times, making eight boxes (see the diagram that follows).

On the chalk board, draw a similar diagram and sketch a simple picture of items from the story or other articles that will be easy for the children to draw. Draw one item in each of the seven boxes. In the eighth box write *Name* so the children will know to write their names in those boxes on their pictures. The children sketch the pictures in the boxes on their own papers and write the beginning or ending sound of the words at the bottom of each box.

- Make a sequence page by folding a large sheet of paper in fourths. Have each student illustrate the four main parts of the story.

Science

- Discuss some characteristics of insects

  Most insects fly
  Insects have three parts
  Insects lay eggs
  Insects go through a metamorphosis

- *Metamorphosis:* Define the word. On a sheet of paper have students write the word and give a definition in their own words, then illustrate it.

- More able learners may wish to read books on insects and informally report their findings to the class. Allow children to decide the depth of their research.

Math

- Place a calendar in the caterpillar corner. At the beginning of each day discuss what is happening in the caterpillar's life cycle as you discuss the day in September.

- Introduce the term *symmetry*. Help children develop an awareness of the symmetry of insects. Use the term frequently.

- Using the various colors that butterflies can be, keep a record of different-colored butterflies the children have seen by drawing a graph.

- Using word cards with the days of the week written on them, discuss the sequence of events in *The Very Hungry Caterpillar*. Mix the cards and have the children place them in proper sequence.

- Have children match the numbers used in the story to number words.

Social Studies

Discuss the migration of the monarch butterfly. Trace the routes on a map.

> Would they have to fly over water?
> How long would the migration take?

Foreign Language

Introduce some of the corresponding vocabulary:

> the days of the week
> number words to ten
> the word for *butterfly*

Music

Play *Papillons* by Robert Schumann as the children arrive in the morning and in the background when it is appropriate during the day. *Papillons* is a collection of short piano pieces. Choose one or two as focal points for this activity. After the children are familiar with the chosen selection, have them act out the emergence of a butterfly with the music in the background. Repeat the activity several times. Students may feel shy at first, but as their creative movements are met with approval and encouraged, they will become less inhibited.

Art

Materials

drawing paper

colored chalk

At the end of the week give the children colored chalk and a large piece of paper. Play *Papillons* and have them draw to the music. Encourage them to use color and line instead of shape to express their feelings. Since young children are accustomed to thinking in terms of shape, it may take several sessions for this activity to be successful. Examples of artists' works that express ideas in free form may help.

Week 2: Overview

Instructional Books

Are You a Ladybug? by Brian and Jillian Cutting
Caterpillar Diary by David Drew
Living or Not Living by Judith Halloway and Clive Harper

Related Titles

The Grouchy Ladybug by Eric Carle
A Small World by Brian and Jillian Cutting

Poems

"Ladybug" by Joan Walsh Anglund
"Butterfly" by Hilda Conkling
"An Insect Has Three Parts" by Marjorie Keiper
"The Butterfly Jar" by Jeff Moss

Music

Papillons by Robert Schumann

Objectives

1. **Phonetic skills**
   Review short and long o
   Introduce short u

2. **Structural analysis**
   Review nouns
3. **Punctuation**
   Introduce concept of a sentence and use of capital letters and periods

Materials

Word cards for vocabulary

Newsprint

Chart paper, 12 by 18 inches

Poetry and Skills Session

DAY 1

"Butterfly"

Step 1: Read the poem aloud to your students several times.
Step 2: Review the sounds of short and long o. Identify words in the poem with these sounds.
Step 3: Introduce the sound of short u. Give numerous examples and ask the children to contribute others.
Step 4: As you read the poem again, have students listen for words that have the sounds you are studying, emphasizing those words.
Step 5: Reread the poem for pleasure.
Step 6: Distribute copies for students' poetry notebooks.

DAY 2

"Ladybug"

Step 1: Introduce the poem and read it several times aloud to the children.
Step 2: Ask different students to locate words that contain a short u sound.
Step 3: Identify a noun in the poem and define *noun*.
Step 4: Elaborate by asking the students to name all the nouns they can think of. They can look around the room and name all the things they see. Make them think even harder by asking them to name things they cannot see, such as air, odors, germs, and so on. If you and your students approach this activity with humor, it can be an excellent thinking activity.

One discussion, based on the concept that a noun is anything you can see, took a delightful turn when the teacher asked the students to think of things she was wearing that they could not see. The children began with the suggestion "Underwear!" After the giggles subsided, the class agreed that, indeed, underwear is a noun. The question that followed was, "What other things could I be wearing that you cannot see?" The children then began naming make-up, hair spray, deodorant, hand lotion, and so on. The thinking that was evoked by this exercise helped the students become aware of elements in the environment that may not be obvious, which led them to, "What is on the playground that you cannot see?" The responses ranged from grass seed to fertilizer to rain. A game evolved and the class began asking the question, "What is a _____ wearing that you cannot see?" It certainly became a creative activity!

Depending on time and your patience, this discussion can become a delightful activity that can be extended into other areas. It is a great time filler when waiting for a special teacher to arrive or the few minutes before time to go to lunch. Ask questions such as, "What would an astronaut (doctor, storekeeper, baby sitter, and so on) be wearing that you could not see?"

Step 5: Ask students to find name words (nouns) in today's poem. Circle the words with a washable pen on the laminated copy or have the students circle the words.

Step 6: Reread the poem for pleasure and distribute copies for the students' poetry books.

DAY 3

"The Butterfly Jar"

Step 1: Read the poem aloud to the children several times.

Step 2: Discuss the content of the poem, leading the children to observe that poetry is written differently from prose.

Step 3: Discuss the use of capital letters.

Step 4: If some children note that capitals letters are used differently in poetry than in prose, take the time to explore this concept.

Step 5: Reread the poem for pleasure and distribute copies to be illustrated for student books.

DAY 4

"An Insect Has Three Parts"

The words to this poem, written by Marjorie Keiper, are sung to the tune of "The Farmer in the Dell."

An insect has three parts,
An insect has three parts.
Head, thorax, abdomen,
An insect has three parts.

An insect has six legs,
An insect has six legs.
Joined to the thorax,
An insect has six legs.

A spider has eight legs,
A spider has eight legs.
A spider's not an insect
It's an arachnid.

Step 1: Sing this song with the children several times.
Step 2: Ask the children to circle the name words (nouns) in the poem with a washable pen.
Step 3: Review the vowel sounds.
Step 4: Sing the song a final time and distribute copies to be illustrated.

DAY 5

The students have enough poems to begin a weekly session of reading aloud from their collections. Ask each child to choose a poem to read to the class. Allow students to read in pairs or small groups if they wish. During these sessions the poetry should be used for pleasure rather than instruction.

Reading Instruction

DAY 1

Caterpillar Diary

Shared Reading

Step 1: Introduce the story using the big book.

Step 2: Have the students make predictions about the story. Encourage them to use visual clues to predict the factual content.

Step 3: Compare and contrast the cover with that of *The Very Hungry Caterpillar*.

Step 4: Discuss the factual differences between the two caterpillars.

Step 5: Read the book to the class, pausing on each page to discuss the information.

Step 6: Look carefully at the photographs to gather information about antennae, legs, symmetry of wings, cocoon, and other elements.

Small Group Instruction

The purpose of this session is to enjoy the book and discuss the information.

Step 1: Invite the students to come to the reading area in mixed groups.

Step 2: Ask the groups to select from the story some vocabulary words they would like to learn.

Step 3: Write these words on the board and have the children find the words in the book. (Before the next session transfer these words to word cards.)

Step 4: At the end of the session have children fold a 12-by-18-inch sheet of newsprint three times to form eight boxes.

Step 5: Open the paper.

Step 6: Direct the students to cut along the folded lines on the top half only. They will write a word on the top part, lift it, and illustrate the word on the under part. These books are called "flip books." (See diagram on p. 19)

DAY 2

Caterpillar Diary

Shared Reading

Step 1: Lead the children in a discussion of *Caterpillar Diary*. Ask them the following questions:

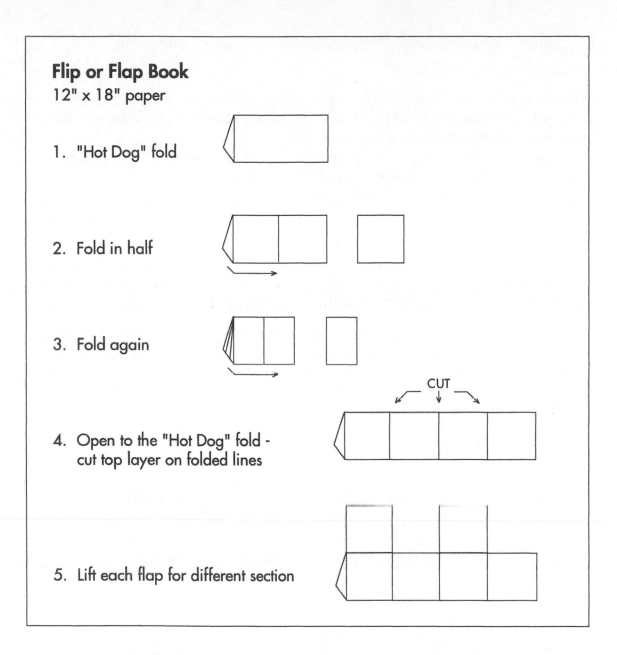

Flip or Flap Book
12" x 18" paper

1. "Hot Dog" fold

2. Fold in half

3. Fold again

4. Open to the "Hot Dog" fold -
   cut top layer on folded lines

   CUT

5. Lift each flap for different section

- What have they learned from it?
- How does it differ from *The Very Hungry Caterpillar?* Have them list the differences and similarities.

Step 2: Introduce the concept of sentences. Capital letters are the signal that a new sentence, or thought, is beginning. The period is placed at the end of the sentence.

Step 3: Give the children time to identify the sentences on several of the pages. Read the sentences in a variety of ways to help the children understand the importance of punctuation.

Step 4:   Reread the story, taking time to discuss the photographs.

Small Group Instruction

EL: Have each student take turns choosing words from the vocabulary cards until all words have been read. Allow each student to show his or her word to the group, read it, and use it in a sentence.

Read *Caterpillar Diary* with the group as a choral reading. This technique allows all children to participate without knowing all the words. It also allows the teacher to identify those children who need extra assistance. It may help young children to use a marker as they read, which also shows instantly who is reading successfully.

TL: Follow the same procedure as described in the EL section. Using directed reading strategies, read the book together offering assistance as needed. Note any words that cause students difficulty that are not included on the vocabulary cards.

AL: Follow the same vocabulary word procedure described in the EL and TL sections. Have the students read silently, a page at a time, offering assistance as needed. Briefly discuss the content of each page to check their comprehension.

DAY 3

Caterpillar Diary

Shared Reading

Step 1:   Look at the pictures on each page and have the children make up conversations for the insects to have. For example, the insects in the pictures could be talking to the person writing the book.

Step 2:   The conversations could be written on paper and placed on the pictures, changing the pictures into cartoons.

Step 3:   Encourage students to use the scientific terms that you have presented.

Small Group Instruction

EL: Review the selected vocabulary. Have individuals select some part of the book to read aloud. Ask them to practice by reading their parts silently, and offer them help as needed. Then have them read their parts to others in the group.

TL: Ask the following questions and have the students locate the sentences that contain the answers:

- Why did the author write the book? (3)

- How does the author know the creature was a moth? (13)

- How does the author know when the caterpillar is ready to spin its cocoon? (9)

- When does the author first realize the caterpillar is going to be a moth? (16)
- What is the caterpillar's first meal? (5)
- What are false eyes and why are they important? (14)
- How long is the pupa in the cocoon? (11)

AL: Have students read *Living or Not Living* silently and discuss the content. Ask them to compare this book with *Caterpillar Diary*. Encourage students to tell how the authors of these two books relate factual information. Contrast their use of such information with the way in which Eric Carle used similar information.

DAY 4

Are You a Ladybug?

Shared Reading

Step 1: Introduce *Are You a Ladybug?*

Step 2: Compare and contrast this book with *Caterpillar Diary* and *The Very Hungry Caterpillar*.

Step 3: Lead the students to see the difference between photographs, realistic illustrations, and Eric Carle's illustrations.

Step 4: Read the book aloud and discuss the information it contains.

Small Group Instruction

Step 1: Place the children in mixed groups for this activity.

Step 2: Ask the students to find the names of insects included in the story and write them on the board.

Step 3: Have the groups read the story aloud with half of each group asking "Are you a ladybug?" and the others reading the response.

Step 4: Read the story again, reversing roles.

Step 5: Have students fold a sheet of paper twice (into fourths), write the name of a different insect in each box, and illustrate the words. Cut the boxes apart and staple the pages into a small book.

DAY 5

Shared Reading

This discussion should focus on the information found in the books that have been read by and to the children.

Step 1: Using a large chart paper, write the names of insects and record information about each beside its name.

Step 2: Encourage the children to discuss the data they have gathered during these two weeks.

Step 3: Have the students form several smaller groups; approximately four per group is a workable number. Give each group a sheet of 12-by-18-inch paper and instruct them to make a poster about one of the insects they have been studying. They should

> Name and draw a large picture of the insect.
> Write several facts about it.
> Include the name of their team on the poster.

Step 4: Take time to help them plan the steps necessary to accomplish the assignment. The first few times children attempt an assignment of this nature they may have trouble working together; with practice they will learn to cooperate.

Step 5: Allow students to use books about insects to gather information and to help spell words. Circulate among the children while they are working, encouraging and assisting them as needed.

Step 6: Have each group share their poster with the class. Comment in a positive way on the strengths of each poster.

Step 7: Display the finished posters in a prominent place.

Independent Activities

Materials Needed

Caterpillar booklets (see p. 23)

Paper plates or large circles

Shape booklets

White paper with large circle pattern

Black paper with a pattern slightly larger than the white circle

Black paper with large circle pattern

Red paper using the same circle pattern as previous item

Paper brads

Manila paper

Tag board

Tongue depressors

Extension Activities

- Have students make a caterpillar book by folding a long strip of paper like an accordion. Holding the folded paper together, round one edge and paste a large circle on one end. When unfolded, the strip looks like a caterpillar. Students will write and illustrate a story using each section as a page.

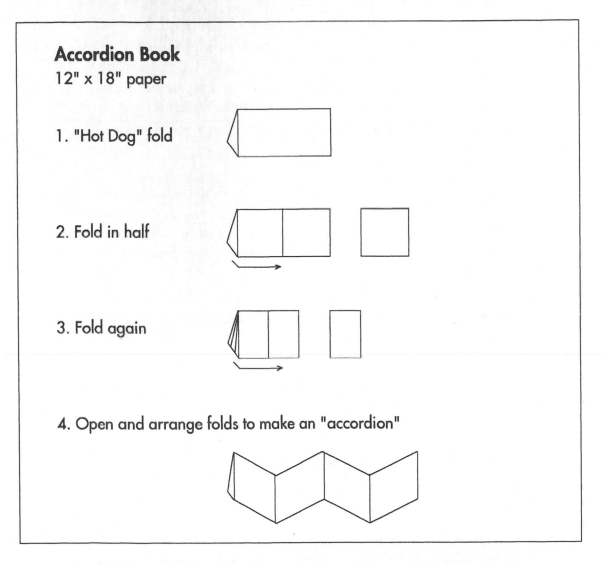

Accordion Book
12" x 18" paper

1. "Hot Dog" fold

2. Fold in half

3. Fold again

4. Open and arrange folds to make an "accordion"

- Have students draw lines on a paper plate or large circle to divide it into fourths. They will write a story about a caterpillar who became a butterfly, with each fourth telling of a stage of the life cycle.

- Have students cut sheets of paper into the shape of an insect. They will make a book in that shape, drawing a different insect and recording three or facts about the insect on each page.

- Students will make a lady bug by drawing a large circle on black paper (a paper plate makes a good pattern). They form the head by adding a smaller half circle to the larger one. On red paper, they will draw a large circle the same size as the body, fold it in half, and cut along the folded line. They will use a paper brad to attach these two half circles to the body to form the wings, then add black spots to the wings. Remind students about symmetry.

- Cut out a large circle of white paper for each child. The children will fold the circles into fourths and draw lines on the folded lines to make the divisions clear. They will choose an insect and illustrate its life cycle, one stage in each fourth: egg, larvae, pupa, adult. Paste the circles on larger circles of black paper, and attach tongue depressors to make the drawings look like magnifying glasses.

Small Group and Center Activities

- Let each child draw a large picture of an insect, clearly showing the parts. Paste the drawings on pieces of tag board or heavy paper. Laminate the pictures. Children will cut their pictures into puzzle pieces, place the pieces in envelopes labeled with the names of the insects and the students. Place the puzzles in a box so students can share them.

- Fold a large piece of manila drawing paper in half. Label one side "moth" and the other "butterfly." The students then illustrate the differences between the two insects.

- Fold paper as in the previous activity and label the halves "harmful insects" and "helpful insects." The students draw pictures under the appropriate headings and label the insects.

- Have students illustrate "symmetrical" by folding a piece of paper in half, cutting it into the shape of wings and, either drawing or using the cut paper, creating symmetrical designs. Display these on a bulletin board with a "symmetrical" title.

- Display a number of insect and sea animal books. Ask the students to find pictures of animals that have exoskeletons. Insects will, of course, be included, and by perusing the ocean life books they should discover that shrimp, lobsters, snails, and crab are among other animals that fall in this category. Have students draw and cut out pictures and label them; display the results on a bulletin board.

Science

- Identify similarities and differences between moths and butterflies:

antennae	habits
size	cocoon
color	**chrysalis**

- Identify parts of an insect:

  antennae
  thorax
  abdomen

- Identify and read information about

  praying mantis
  bee
  spider

Discuss why each of these is or is not an insect.

- If funds allow, purchase a butterfly box. These include a coupon for butterfly caterpillars that arrive live, in a compound that furnishes the necessary food until they form the chrysalis. The caterpillars attach themselves to the paper that covers the top of the container, which you transfer to the butterfly box. In approximately two weeks the butterflies emerge from the cocoon. It is a thrilling event for young children who have been reading about this process.

Our students watch this process each fall during the insect unit. They debate many questions during this time. They talk about what the insects are eating and the changes in the chrysalis toward the end of their metamorphosis. One year we had Painted Lady butterflies and the children noticed that metallic dots appeared on the chrysalis several days before the butterflies emerged.

The students became so excited about the caterpillars that they began capturing every one they saw. At one time there were nine in our butterfly box. The children brought in leaves each day to feed them. One caterpillar, quite different from the others, did not find any of the leaves compatible with its needs and eventually died. The children then discussed the ethics of keeping these small animals and ultimately decided to free all of them.

Math

- Using the pictures in *Caterpillar Diary* and *Are You a Ladybug?* have student observe the symmetry of the markings on the wings and the symmetry evident in other parts of the insect.

  What other examples of symmetry in insects can they find?

- Introduce simple addition facts using the spots on a ladybug's wings.

Social Studies

Discuss the importance of insects to farmers. Discuss pollination, harmful insects, and helpful insects, including the impact of chemical insect control on the environment as opposed to farmers' need to protect crops from destructive bugs. Introduce the concept of biological control, such as using ladybugs to control aphids, as part of organic farming.

Foreign Language

Review the vocabulary that has been introduced. Have students begin a dictionary, including *flower, honey, help,* and so on, and have them illustrate each word. Continue adding to the basic vocabulary bank of insect words.

Music

The children will be familiar with *Papillons* by now. As you play the music describe a butterfly emerging from a cocoon and have students imagine how it would feel. Repeat and have students mime the emergence using only one hand. Repeat and have them mime using their whole body.

Next, have students pretend to be butterflies that have just emerged. They spread their wings, then soar into the air and are lifted on wind currents. Imagine what it would be like for a butterfly to look down on the Earth.

Art

Materials

tree branch

construction paper

colored tissue paper

glue

glitter (optional)

pipe cleaners

Designate a corner as the insect area and set up the tree branch. (If you can't find a tree branch large enough, a bulletin board could serve the same purpose.) Encourage children to make insects out of different materials to hang on the tree.

Have the students draw the outline of a large butterfly on paper, paint small areas with liquid glue, and cover the butterflies with small squares of colored tissue paper. After the glue has dried, students can cut out the butterflies, add antennae, use the creations in imagery activities, and hang them on the tree.

Week 3: Overview

Instructional Books

I Was Walking Down the Road by Sarah E. Barchas
The Message of the Dance by Ann Coleridge

Related Titles

"I can't," said the ant by Polly Cameron (to be read aloud)
In the Tall, Tall Grass by Denice Fleming
Two Bad Ants by Chris Van Allsburg (to be read aloud)

Poems

"Joyful" by Rose Burgunder
"September" by Maurice Sendak

Music

Flight of the Bumblebee by Rimsky-Korsakov

Objectives

1. **Phonetic skills**
   Introduce short and long e
2. **Structural analysis**
   Identify rhyming words
3. **Comprehension**
   Review nouns
   Introduce verbs
   Identify sentences

4. **Punctuation**
    Capitals
    Periods

Materials

Vowel cards

Chart paper

Paper with the following sentence printed on it:

"I was _____ on a _____ and I saw a _____."
(for emergent readers or children who have difficulty writing).

Accordion books (see p. 23)

Poetry and Skills Session

DAY 1

"Joyful"

Step 1: Read the poem aloud once to the class and then several times all together.
Step 2: Introduce long e.
Step 3: Have the children identify and mark words that have the long e sound.
Step 4: Ask the children to find in the poem words with the long e sound and begin a list of these words.
Step 5: Read the poem a final time for pleasure.
Step 6: Distribute copies for the children to illustrate and place in their poetry books.

DAY 2

"Joyful"

Step 1: Reread the poem and review the vowel sounds.
Step 2: Ask the students to name words that have these sounds and add the words to the list. (Children who are having difficulty with this concept should be grouped together during small group sessions for extra help. As these children master the sound, group them for different purposes.)

Step 3: Ask the children to identify the nouns in the poem.

Step 4: Introduce verbs to the class.

Step 5: Ask for a volunteer to stand and move around the room. Ask others to tell what the child is doing: walk, talk, skip, etc. Record their responses.

Step 6: Explain that these words are doing words (verbs). Encourage the children to give other examples of verbs and record the words. Students may wish to focus on verbs that are related to insects.

Step 7: Read the poem a final time for pleasure.

DAY 3

"September"

Step 1: Introduce the poem by reading it to the class.

Step 2: Allow the students to play with the rhythm of the words. They will especially enjoy the pattern of "_____ once, _____ twice, _____ chicken soup with rice."

Step 3: Encourage students to vary these lines.

Step 4: Ask the children to identify the verb in the poem (*ride*).

Step 5: Invite the students to list other verbs.

Step 6: Identify the nouns in the poem.

Step 7: Read the poem several more times before ending the session.

Step 8: Distribute copies for the children to illustrate and add to their poetry notebooks.

DAY 4

"September"

Step 1: Reread the poem, allowing time for comments and discussion.

Step 2: Introduce short e. Offer several examples and ask the students to contribute their own.

Step 3: Identify words in the poems that have this sound.

Step 4: Record the words.

Step 5: Continue playing with the final rhyme. The children quickly pick up on this exercise and will use it spontaneously during the day.

DAY 5

Step 1: Reread the poems that have been introduced.

Step 2: Allow time for students to enjoy each poem as it is read by the group.

Step 3: Give the class colored cards with one vowel printed on each. Use one color, such as red, for short vowels and another color, perhaps green, for the long vowels.

Step 4: Choose a leader to say a word; the children hold up the card with the appropriate sound. (The color coding and the letter allow for instant evaluation of selections.)

Step 5: As the children respond make note of those who are having problems and group them for reteaching at a later time.

Reading Instruction

DAY 1

The Message of the Dance

Shared Reading

This book will be difficult for the children to read individually, but it offers excellent information about bees and should be used with the whole class.

Step 1: Read the title and ask students to predict what the story is about.

Step 2: Read the book, allowing students ample time to discuss the illustrations and information on each page. It will probably take two sessions to complete this step.

Small Group Instruction

Step 1: Place students in heterogeneous groups and call the groups one at a time to the reading area.

Step 2: Read a page at a time of the first half of the story. It may help the students to use markers to follow the words as you read the book.

Step 3: Encourage any who feel comfortable with the vocabulary to read with you.

Step 4: Have children do the following activities:

- Answer the question, "How many times does 'Lizzie' appear on a designated page?"

- Find a word with one of the vowels we have discussed.

- Point to words you know.

- Discuss in more depth the illustrations and information.

- Begin a bee fact chart.

Step 5: Allow the small groups to tell what they have learned about bees. They may share information they knew before reading the book.

DAY 2

Follow the same plan as for Day 1, reading the second half of the book. Continue discussing as you read. Encourage observations about the pattern of the honeycomb and stages of growth of the insects.

DAY 3

I Was Walking Down the Road

Shared Reading

Step 1: Introduce the story to the class. Ask students to predict what the book is about.

Step 2: Compare the illustrations to those in *The Message of the Dance*.

Step 3: Read the book with the whole class.

Small Group Instruction

Step 1: Again call the children in heterogeneous groups.

Step 2: Take turns reading the text. Suggest that the children form two smaller groups to read the story. Allow them to arrange the groups. One group reads the first two lines, the other, the rest of the page:

First Group
I was looking for my mitten
when I saw a little kitten.

Second Group
I caught it,
I picked it up.
I put it in a cage.

Step 3: Reverse the procedure so everyone has an opportunity to read all the text.

DAY 4

I Was Walking Down the Road

Shared Reading

Step 1: Reread the story with the group.

Step 2: Encourage children to identify rhyming words.

Step 3: Choose two or three words as time allows and expand the word family.

Step 4: Encourage the children to use these words in sentences.

Step 1: Place children in groups according to instructional need.

Step 2: During the first part of the session give attention to the needs of the group then allow the children to read aloud in pairs.

Step 3: Ask the children to think of new animals and locations, for example, *dog, bog; giraffe, raft;* etc.

Step 4: Make up new parts for the story. Record some of these on chart paper.

DAY 5

I Was Walking Down the Road

Shared Reading

Step 1: Conduct a general discussion of the book. Ask the children to identify their favorite parts.

Step 2: Give the children accordion books and have them write their own version of the story.

Step 3: Use the reading block for this activity.

Step 4: As you offer individual assistance, remind the children to use capital letters and periods.

Step 5: Write the form of the story on the board to help children who are not yet comfortable writing independently.

"I was _____ on a _____ and I saw a _____.
I caught it. I picked it up. I put it in a cage."

For very young children for whom writing is still difficult, print the sentence on paper, copy it, then cut apart and glue the sheets in the previously prepared booklets. Students can then add the appropriate words to complete the story.

Step 6: Have students illustrate and share the books at the end of the period. Encourage the students to follow these steps:

Read the book to yourself; correct any errors you catch.

Read the book to a friend; correct any errors he or she catches.

Read the book to your teacher; correct any errors she or he notices.

Independent Activities

Materials Needed

newsprint

black and brown construction paper

small books for students to use

paper with connecting pentagons

newspaper torn into small pieces

balloons or other forms for insect bodies

liquid starch

Extension Activities

- Have children make flip books of rhyming words and illustrate the words.

- Place the children in small groups or have them choose small groups. They will act out *I Was Walking Down the Road*. Have the class guess the animal the group is depicting and the location in which it was found.

- Have students make a bee verb book. On the front they will write, "A bee can . . . " Then on each of the following pages they will write a word that a bee can do: buzz, fly, make honey, dance. They will illustrate each page.

- Students will make an insect comparison page. The children choose two insects they wish to compare and write sentences, for example, "A bee is like a butterfly because they both like flowers, carry pollen on their legs, and help people." Encourage the children to think of many ways in which different insects are similar. They should illustrate their comparison in some way.

- Students will illustrate the dances of the bees that are displayed in *The Message of the Dance*. Let the children use a piece of dark paper and draw the path of the dance with chalk. They label the "message" at the bottom of the paper.

Small Group and Center Activities

- Give the children a sheet that has large connecting pentagons on it to represent a bee hive. Have them fill in the shapes with life in a bee hive. Stress the patterning as shown on page 6 of the text.

- Fold a strip of drawing paper, 18 by 6 inches, into fourths. Play *Flight of the Bumblebee* and have students draw pictures of the story suggested by the music. They should give the story a beginning, a middle, and an end in sections 2, 3, and 4, respectively. Each student will write the name of the story and his or her name as author and illustrator in the first section.

- Cut light brown construction paper into 18-by-6-inch strips. Fold the strips into thirds then the folded pieces in half, making six sections. Open and refold so all the folded lines go in the same direction. Tape the end edges together, forming a hexagon. Stack the "cells" to make a class "bee hive". Have the children draw, color, and cut out bees in various stages of the life cycle. Place them in the hive. Make papier mâché bees for the hive.

- Make bees with manila paper and paste them together as described in the butterfly activity in Week 1.

Science

- Focus on the life cycle of the bee.

- Compare and contrast the bee with other insects.

- Discuss bees' usefulness to humans.

- Look at an illustration of parts of a plant

  Locate pollen
  Locate nectar

- Look at a picture of a bee. Find the pollen sacks on the legs.

Math

Step 1: Write the days of the week and number words on cards.
Step 2: Have each student draw a card for a day of the week and a corresponding number word.

Step 3: Arrange the days of the week in sequence.

Step 4: Change the theme to "A Very Hungry Bee." Have each child tell how many items the bee ate on each day of the week. Use number words randomly. Encourage diversity and creative thinking. Accept all responses with a positive attitude.

Patterns

- Have children look for examples of patterns in nature. Discuss differences between symmetry and patterns.

- Make a graph of the number of insects identified by the students.

Social Studies

What food do we get from animals?

Have the children make a mural of animals and food we get from them. Use a combination of drawing and collage.

Foreign Language

Focus on the French names of animals. Add some of these to the illustrated dictionary or card file.

Music and Art

Materials

drawing paper

crayons or chalk

Listen to *Flight of the Bumblebee* by Rimsky-Korsakov several times during the week. During one session give the children large sheets of paper and have them draw the flight of the bee. At the end ask them to look at the lines and color in shapes that relate to their knowledge of the bees. They might find a hive cell, a flower, a hive, a wing, etc.

Week 4: Overview

Instructional Books

I Know an Old Lady Who Swallowed a Fly by Rose Bonne
Have You Seen My Cat? by Eric Carle
Rooster's Off to See the World by Eric Carle
The Very Busy Spider by Eric Carle (to be read aloud)
Insects Are Animals by Judith Halloway and Clive Harper
The Giant Jam Sandwich by John V. Lord (to be read aloud)
I Love Spiders by John Parker

Related Titles

Other Eric Carle titles (to be read aloud)
I Went Walking by Sue Williams

Poems

"Wasps," by Dorothy Aldis
"The Bug," by Marjorie Barrows

Music

Flight of the Bumblebee
Papillons

Objectives

1. **Phonetic Skills**
   Review and drill short o and u, long o
2. **Structural analysis**
   Rhyming words
3. **Comprehension**
   Predict outcomes
   Sequence
   Verbs
   Classification
   Introduction of adjectives

Materials

Vocabulary cards

Drawing paper, 12 by 18 inches

Writing paper

Poetry and Skills Session

DAY 1

"Wasps"

Step 1: Introduce the poem and read it aloud several times for enjoyment.
Step 2: Discuss wasps; compare and contrast them with other insects.
Step 3: Review the vowel sounds introduced and ask the students to identify them in the poem.
Step 4: Read the poem a final time for enjoyment.
Step 5: Distribute copies for the children to illustrate and add to their poetry notebooks.

DAY 2

"Wasps"

Step 1: Reread the poem and allow time for comments and discussion.
Step 2: Have students identify rhyming words.
Step 3: Review nouns and verbs and have students identify them in the poem.
Step 4: Read the poem a final time for pleasure.

DAY 3

"The Bug"

Step 1: Introduce the poem and ask the children to point out words they know.
Step 2: Read the poem with the whole class.
Step 3: Briefly review the long and short vowels.
Step 4: Distribute copies for the children to illustrate and add to their poetry notebooks.

DAY 4

"The Bug"

Step 1: Have students identify rhyming words.
Step 2: Based on suggestions from the group, change the beginning sound of bug to create a word family. Example: *hug, rug, mug.* Record these on a large outline of a bug.
Step 3: Encourage the children to make up silly sentences using as many "ug" words as possible.

DAY 5

Let the children choose poems they will read aloud, either solo or with a friend. This should be a session for the enjoyment of poetry. If remediation is necessary, make notes and address these needs at another time.

Reading Instruction

DAY 1

I Love Spiders

Shared Reading

Step 1: Have students predict what the story is about and allow time for them to discuss whether they agree with the title.

Step 2: Discuss the differences between spiders and insects.

Step 3: Read the book together and discuss the accuracy of students' predictions.

Small Group Instruction

Use this time to address remediation needs. Call the children according to individual needs.

- Use *I Love Spiders* to strengthen decoding skills.

- Read the story for pleasure, pairing stronger and emergent readers.

- Make vocabulary cards for the words that are new to the children.

DAY 2

I Love Spiders

Shared Reading

Step 1: Pass out the vocabulary cards that have been made for the story.

Step 2: Cover these words in the story and have children supply the words as the story is read.

Step 3: Ask each child to make up a sentence using the word he or she holds.

Small Group Instruction

EL: Review and drill with the vocabulary words.

Step 1: Write sentences on the board with words missing and have the children supply the correct word.

Step 2: Read each sentence out loud.

Step 3: Ask each child to select a page in the book to read orally.

Step 4: Make note of words that are difficult for the children.

Step 5: At the end of the oral reading write all of these words on the board. This practice does not single out a child who misses some words; it takes the pressure off students who feel they need to know all the words.

Step 6: Ask the students to select four words they would like to learn and to write these words in each section of a paper they have folded into fourths.

Step 7: Have students illustrate the word and write a sentence using it. The boxes can be cut apart to make a "study book".

TL: Reread *I Love Spiders*.

Step 1: Have the students select two vocabulary word cards, find the words in the text, and read that portion of the book aloud.

Step 2: Have students select four vocabulary words to illustrate, as you did with the previous group.

AL: Read *I Know An Old Lady* . . . .

Step 1: Encourage the children to enjoy the rhyme.

Step 2: Ask the students to locate vocabulary common to this and *I Love Spiders*.

DAY 3

The Giant Jam Sandwich

Shared Reading

Step 1: Introduce the story to the class and have students try to predict what will happen.

Step 2: Read the book to the class.

Step 3: Discuss illustrations, fact, and fiction in the story.

Step 4: Ask the class to identify insects that are harmful. How are they controlled? The discussion should include environmental issues. Encourage the children to draw on knowledge acquired during the study.

Small Group Instruction

EL: *I Love Spiders*

Step 1: Ask the children to look through the book and find all the words that tell something about spiders.

Step 2: Write these words on the board. Tell the children that these are "describing words" (adjectives). Do not expect mastery of this concept at this time.

Step 3: Ask for other words that would describe a spider. Write these words on the board.

Step 4: Distribute 12-by-18-inch sheets of paper; have the children fold them to make flip books. They will then choose four of the describing words, combine them with *spider,* write the phrase on the outside of the paper, and illustrate it on the underside.

TL: *Have You Seen My Cat?*

Step 1: Introduce the book to the group.

Step 2: Read the book together, using directed reading strategies.

Step 3: Ask the children to name all the animals in the story, writing the names of the animals on the board as children identify them.

Step 4: Discuss different ways these animals could be categorized: animals with stripes, cats, meat eaters, and so on.

Step 5: Tell the group to make flip books with names of the animals on the outside, a short sentence about each on the inside, and an illustration.

AL: *Rooster's Off to See the World*

Step 1: Distribute copies of the book and allow time for students to comment. They should recognize Eric Carle's style.

Step 2: Have students predict what will happen in the story.

Step 3: Proceed, using directed reading strategies.

Step 4: Compare and contrast the story with other Eric Carle titles.

DAY 4

Insects Are Animals

Shared Reading

Review all characteristics of insects. Have students contrast and compare these characteristics with what they know about other animals. Compare and contrast different insects. Read the book together.

Small Group Instruction

Group students according to need. Reread the story and allow ample time for students to discuss the illustrations. This is a good opportunity to mix students with differing reading abilities. List new vocabulary words on the board. Encourage students to discuss vowels and other decoding strategies.

DAY 5

Shared Reading

The culminating activity for this unit is a general discussion about insects.

Step 1: Summarize the information presented, asking children to tell what they have learned about insects during this study.

Step 2: Inquire about the parts the children especially enjoyed. Allow children to express negative feelings, if they wish.

Step 3: Review *The Giant Jam Sandwich.*

Step 4: Ask the children to think of an undesirable insect. They will write a story describing the pest and how they would get rid of it. Encourage fanciful ideas as well as practical ones.

Suggestions:

• Use the time allotted to reading for this activity. Many children will still be uneasy about writing and this period allows you time to give individual assistance. It is also appropriate for the children to help each other.

• Follow the suggestions in Independent Activity 1.

• Allow time for the students to share their work.

> One year when our students wrote about an undesirable insect one of them came to the final conclusion that they would "call an exterminator then get a new house!"

Suggest the class develop an insect dictionary. Let the students choose words for each letter of the alphabet, then assign each student one or more letters. Give them large pieces of paper on which to write the letter, the word, a sentence, and an illustration. Combine all the work into a class book that everyone can read and enjoy. These books are excellent items to place in a prominent place during open house or conferences. It gives the parents an opportunity to see what is happening in the class.

Allow the children to use the reading period for this activity and offer individualized instruction to children who need help in identified areas.

Independent Activities

Materials

Brown construction paper

Pattern of a large slice of bread

Writing paper

Construction paper

Plastic wrap

String or yarn

Manila folders for riddle book (see p. 43)

Small paper sacks

Black construction paper

Extension Activities

- Ask students to write individual stories, based on *The Giant Jam Sandwich,* about how they would get rid of an insect. Use lined paper in the shape of a slice of bread. Trace this shape on two pieces of brown construction paper and make a "sandwich" book. Have students make small insects from manila paper and paste and glue them to the outside of the book.

- Have students write a story based on *I Love Spiders*. "I love _____, but I hate _____."

- Have students draw a favorite insect in the center of a large piece of paper and "clouds" around the insect. In each cloud, students will write one fact about the insect.

- Have students compile an A-B-C insect dictionary. Precut the letters, if you wish. Each child will choose a letter and create a page for the book. Combine the pages into a big book.

- Have the children draw a large old lady. Cut a hole for her mouth. Attach a long string to the back of the paper, with the other end coming out of the mouth. Have students draw and cut out items the old lady swallows. Tape these items to the string. They can be pulled from the mouth. Write a story using the sequence of the items. Make a book using the old lady for the cover.

- Students could also draw pictures of the items the old lady swallowed and place them in a window in her stomach. The window could be covered with a clear plastic wrap or the woman could be laminated and the illustrations taped to the back so they are displayed behind the window.

Small Group and Center Activities

- Create a class riddle book.

  Step 1: Give each child a manila folder that has been trimmed so both edges are even. Make two cuts on the center fold and fold this smaller section in the opposite way from the rest of the folder so when the folder is opened, this section pops out (see diagram).

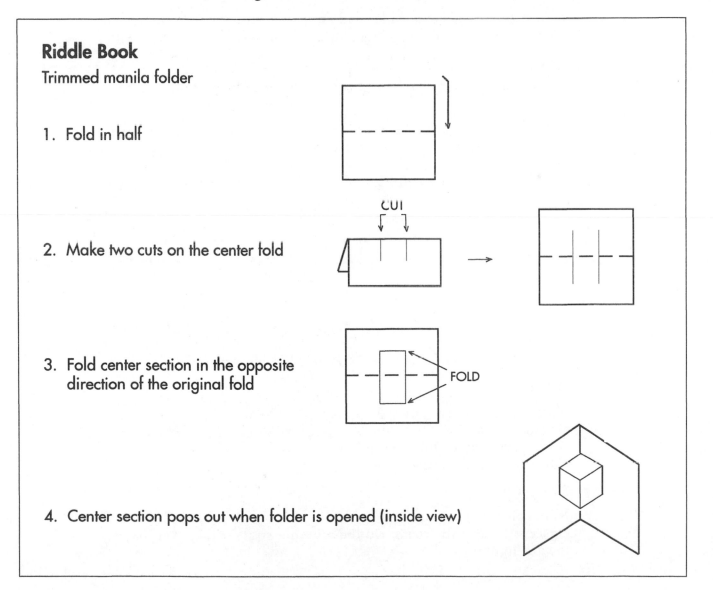

Riddle Book
Trimmed manila folder

1. Fold in half

CUT

2. Make two cuts on the center fold

3. Fold center section in the opposite direction of the original fold

   FOLD

4. Center section pops out when folder is opened (inside view)

Step 2: On the outside of the folder the student writes a riddle the answer to which is the name of an insect. The student cuts out the answer from paper and glues it in the inside of the folder, onto the pop-up part.

Step 3: Have students color a background around the insect.

Step 4: Punch holes in the folders and combine them in a notebook or add covers and hold them together with rings.

- Students could also write insect riddles on small paper sacks. The sack could hold the answer.

- Have students make a spider web by gluing string onto black construction paper. If necessary, reread *The Very Busy Spider* to the class to help them remember how a spider web is formed. Make a spider out of construction paper and glue it to the web.

- Have students make a spider and an insect, glue them to the top of a 12-by-18-inch sheet of manila construction paper, and list the differences between spiders and insects.

- Have students make grouchy books. Provide construction paper that has been cut into 6-by-9-inch pieces. The children write at the bottom of each page, "I get grouchy when . . . " and illustrate the statement. Let them determine how many pages they wish to include. Encourage them to write at least three statements. Combine these pages into small books and let each child design a cover, write the title "The Grouchy (their name)" and print "written and illustrated by . . . "

Science

- Discuss some characteristics of spiders.

  Have students make a chart or Venn diagram that contrasts spiders with insects.
  Have students define and use "arachnid" in a sentence.

- Discuss wasps.

  Note some facts about wasps.
  Discuss nests. Point out that the discovery of paper was based upon the observation of the paper wasp.
  Compare and contrast wasps with bees.

- Discuss flies.

  Note some facts about flies
  Observe flies in the room: Do they fly in a straight line? Do they fly toward light?

Math

Make up story problems based on *The Giant Jam Sandwich*, such as the following: *Five wasps were on the bread eating jam. Some more came. Then there were 8 wasps on the bread. How many wasps joined the first group? 5 + ____ = 8.*

Encourage the students to make up problems and write the corresponding sentences. The illustrations could be completed first and the number sentences added later. This activity is a good one for having children work in pairs.

Social Studies

Discuss the economic issues of too many and too few insects. What is the impact upon plants, animals and humans?

Foreign Language

Continue using insect vocabulary in these classes. Play a game in which you give the name of an insect and a child acts out the insect's behavior.

Music and Art

Play the various musical selections used during the unit. Ask the class to illustrate their favorite. Display the illustrations on a bulletin board with the title and composer of each work. You could place these pictures in a class book after they have been on the board.

Bibliography

Books

Barchas, Sarah E. *I Was Walking Down the Road*. New York: Scholastic, 1975.

Bonne, Rose. *I Know an Old Lady Who Swallowed a Fly*. New York: Scholastic Magazine, 1961.

Cameron, Polly. *"I can't," said the ant*. New York: Scholastic, 1961.

Carle, Eric. *The Very Hungry Caterpillar*. New York: The World Publishing, 1969.

———. *Rooster's Off to See the World*. New York: Scholastic, 1989.

———. *The Grouchy Ladybug*. New York: Scholastic, 1977.

———. *The Very Busy Spider*. New York: Scholastic, 1984.

———. *Animals, Animals*. New York: Scholastic, 1991a.

———. *Dragons, Dragons*. Edited by Laura Whipple. New York: Philomel Books, 1991b.

———. *Have You Seen My Cat?* New York: Scholastic, 1991c.

Coleridge, Ann. *The Message of the Dance.* Cleveland: Modern Curriculum Press, 1989.

Cutting, Brian, and Jillian Cutting. *Are You a Ladybug?* Bothell, Wash.: Thomas C. Wright, 1988a.

———. *A Small World.* Bothell, Wash.: Thomas C. Wright, 1988b.

Drew, David. *Caterpillar Diary.* Crystal Lake, Ill.: Thomas Rigby, 1990.

Fleming, Denise. *In the Tall, Tall Grass.* New York: Scholastic, 1992.

Halloway, Judith, and Clive Harper. *Insects Are Animals.* Cleveland: Modern Curriculum Press, 1990a.

———. *Living or Not Living.* Cleveland: Modern Curriculum Press, 1990b.

Howe, James. *I Wish I Were a Butterfly.* San Diego: Gulliver Books, Harcourt Brace Jovanovich, 1987.

Lord, John V. *The Giant Jam Sandwich.* Columbus, Ohio: Weekly Reader, 1972.

Parker, John. *I Love Spiders.* Auckland, New Zealand: Ashton Scholastic Limited, 1988.

Selsam, Millicent, and Ronald Goor. *Backyard Insects.* New York: Scholastic, 1981.

Van Allsburg, Chris. *Two Bad Ants.* Boston: Houghton Mifflin, 1988.

Williams, Sue. *I Went Walking.* New York: Trumpet Club, 1992.

Poems

Aldis, Dorothy. "Wasps." In Jack Prelutsky, *The Random House Book of Poetry for Children.* New York: Random House, 1983.

Anglund, Joan Walsh. "Ladybug." In Jack Prelutsky, *The Random House Book of Poetry for Children.* New York: Random House, 1983.

Arbuthnot, May Hill, ed. *Time for Poetry Anthology.* Chicago: Scott Foresman, 1951.

Barrows, Marjorie. "The Bug." In Jack Prelutsky, *The Random House Book of Poetry for Children.* New York: Random House, 1983.

"Bug in a Jug." In Jack Prelutsky, *The Random House Book of Poetry for Children.* New York: Random House, 1983.

Burgunder, Rose. "Joyful." In Jack Prelutsky, *The Random House Book of Poetry for Children.* New York: Random House, 1983.

Conkling, Hilda. "Butterfly." In May Hill Arbuthnot, ed., *Time for Poetry Anthology.* Chicago: Scott Foresman, 1951.

de Regniers, Beatrice Schenk. "Keep a Poem In Your Pocket." In Jack Prelutsky, *The Random House Book of Poetry for Children.* New York: Random House, 1983.

Farber, Norma. "Oh the Toe-Test." In Jack Prelutsky, *The Random House Book of Poetry for Children.* New York: Random House, 1983.

Keiper, Marjorie. "An Insect Has Three Parts." Unpublished poem.

Moss, Jeff. "The Butterfly Jar." In Jeff Moss, *The Butterfly Jar*. New York: Bantam, 1989.

Prelutsky, Jack, ed. *The Random House Book of Poetry for Children*. New York: Random House, 1983.

Sendak, Maurice. "September." In *Chicken Soup with Rice,* by Maurice Sendak. New York: Scholastic, 1987.

Video

Eric Carle: Picture Writer. Directed by Rawn Fulton. New York: Putnam Grossett, 1993.

Miscellaneous

de Montreville, Doris, and Elizabeth D. Crawford, eds. *Fourth Book of Junior Authors and Illustrators*. New York: H.H. Wilson, 1978.

Kovacs, Deborah, and James Preller. *Meet the Authors and Illustrators*. New York: Scholastic, 1991.

Norby, Shirley, and Gregory Ryan. *Famous Children's Authors*. Minneapolis: T.S. Denison, 1988.

2
OCTOBER

Theme: Signs of Fall and Halloween

Bill Martin, Jr., is a logical follow-up to September author Eric Carle because of the extensive collaboration between the two on predictable, rhyming literature.

Thematic instruction during the month focuses on signs of fall and Halloween. Columbus Day is addressed through poetry, read-aloud stories, and a creative art project.

Week 1: Overview

Instructional Books

Jump, Frog, Jump by Robert Kalan
Christopher Columbus by Stephen Krensky
In 1492 by Jean Marzillo

Related Titles

Chicka Chicka Boom Boom by Bill Martin, Jr., and John Archambault (to be
  read aloud)
Listen to the Rain by Bill Martin, Jr., and John Archambault (to be read aloud)
Other Bill Martin, Jr., titles, (to be read aloud)

Poems

"What Am I?" by Dorothy Aldis
"The Frog" by Vachel Lindsay
"October" by Maurice Sendak

Music

Danse Macabre by Saint-Saens

Objectives

1. **Phonetic skills**
   Review long e.
   Review short u.
   Review i and o.
   Begin to understand long u.

2. **Structural skills**
   Review and reinforce adjectives.
   Review nouns and verbs.

3. **Punctuation**
   Begin to understand the use of question marks.

4. **Comprehension**
   Review the concept of sequence of events.
   Begin to understand the concept of cause and effect.
   Begin to understand the difference between fact and fiction.

5. **Alphabetical sequence**
   Begin to understand alphabetical sequencing.

Materials

Word cards

the outline of a frog on green construction paper for the vocabulary cards with names of the animals in *Jump, Frog Jump*

Writing materials

Poetry and Skills Session

DAY 1

"October"

Step 1: Read the poem together and compare it to "September."

Step 2: Ask for suggestions to change the word "whoopie." The form of these poems helps the children change words to create their own poems. It stimulates creative thinking.

Step 3: Distribute copies of the poem for your students to illustrate and include in their poetry notebooks.

DAY 2

"The Frog"

Step 1: Read this poem to the children, asking them to listen to the rhythm.

Step 2: Read the poem again. This time encourage the children to move with the poem. They will quickly grasp the meter and repeat with you the words at the end of each line.

Step 3: Ask for volunteers to point out words that are repeated.

Step 4: Relate the rhythm of the poem to the movement of a frog. If space allows, the children might pretend to be frogs, jumping while the poem is read.

DAY 3

"The Frog"

Step 1: Reread the poem together.

Step 2: Locate words that have a long e sound.

Step 3: Review and identify words that contain short o and i.

Step 4: Distribute copies of the poem for your students to illustrate and include in their poetry notebooks.

DAY 4

"What Am I?"

Step 1: Read for enjoyment one or two times.

Step 2: Help the children understand that it is written as a riddle.

Step 3: Pass out the poem. The children might enjoy using orange paper to create a collage illustrating this poem.

Step 4: Introduce question mark.

DAY 5

Read individual free-choice selections for enjoyment. It is appropriate for you to make selections also. (This provides an opportunity for you to determine whether any of the children are failing to complete the illustrations and place them in the notebooks.)

Reading Instruction

DAY 1

Jump, Frog, Jump

Shared Reading

Step 1: Instruct the children to look at the cover and predict what will happen in the story.

Step 2: Record these predictions on a small chalkboard or large sheet of paper.

Step 3: After the story is read, review the predictions and discuss those that were accurate. Take some time to discuss why the predictions that were not part of the story were logical. This helps establish an environment in which children feel free to make suggestions without fear of being "wrong."

Step 4: Review short o as heard in "frog."

Step 5: Review short u as in "jump" and introduce long u.

Step 6: Identify other words in the text that contain these short vowels.

Step 7: Identify rhyming words.

Step 8: Identify nouns and verbs.

Step 9: Review adjectives as "describing" words. Identify adjectives in the story.

Step 10: Compare the life cycle of a frog to the life cycle of a butterfly.

Before the next shared reading session, prepare vocabulary cards. Trace the outline of a frog on green construction paper cards, write a word on each card, and laminate the cards. The words can be placed in a large envelope, labeled with the name of the book, and used year after year. The authors place pieces of magnetic tape on the backs of the word cards and put the cards on the chalkboards. This allows use in a variety of activities.

Small Group Instruction

Step 1: Combine all ability groups for this session. Using small individual copies of the story, reread *Jump, Frog, Jump* orally with the children.

Step 2: Read the text together as a choral reading. Have one group read the text and other students respond "Jump, frog, jump." Give all students the opportunity to read both parts in groups, thus supporting beginning readers.

DAY 2

Jump, Frog, Jump

Shared Reading

Step 1: Review the vocabulary words with the group.

Step 2: Reread the story together, encouraging dramatization of the line, "Jump, frog, jump!"

Step 3: Distribute the cards on which the main characters are written: *snake, turtle, fish,* etc. Ask the children holding these cards to arrange themselves in the sequence in which they appear in the story.

Step 4: Briefly review and reinforce phonetic skills as needed by the group.

EL: Vocabulary drill is important for this group. Begin the session by going over the word cards. Ask each child to choose a page to read aloud.

Use *cloze* activities to reinforce vocabulary.

TL:

Step 1: Match rhyming words with "frog" vocabulary. Choose one of the words and make a word family. Examples: *frog, log, hog, bog.*

Step 2: Ask the students to make up sentences using two or more of the words. Example: "I saw a frog on a log in the bog."

Step 3: Let the children read the story orally.

AL:

Step 1: Using the vocabulary cards, have the students match each animal with its target. Example: the "frog" tried to catch the "fly."

Step 2: Discuss the difference in motives between the animals catching other animals and the boys catching the frog. Encourage the children to think about the pros and cons of the activity: Would there be justification for this? What if the frog were needed for a science project? What if it were needed for food? Are there other reasons that justify their actions?

DAY 3

Shared Reading

Choose a book by Bill Martin, Jr., from the suggested reading list. Read it to the group and discuss the story. Help the children "discover" that Bill Martin, Jr., writes the stories and others do the illustrations.

Small Group Instruction

At this time, many skills have been introduced. Because some of the children will have mastered the sounds of vowels quickly while others need more reinforcement, it is appropriate for them to be arranged in small groups according to individual needs.

Use this session to reinforce the following skills according to individual needs:

- In the text, find words that have the target short and long vowels.

- Identify nouns, verbs, and adjectives.

- Discuss punctuation.

- Decide what could really happen in this story and what could not happen.

- Discuss whether the boys should have caught and kept the frog. Why or why not?

DAY 4

Shared Reading

Read another Bill Martin, Jr. book and compare the story to the one read during the previous session. Dr. Martin has frequently collaborated with Eric Carle and John Archambault. The students will enjoy identifying these illustrators.

Small Group Instruction

EL:

Step 1: Review the vocabulary words by placing them on the table (or on the chalkboard if they are magnetized) and then asking individuals to choose a word and use it in a sentence.

Step 2: Arrange the words into groups according to parts of speech.

Step 3: Ask students to choose a word, find it in the story, and read that page orally.

TL:
    Step 1: Alphabetize vocabulary cards.
    Step 2: Review vocabulary or skills from the week's instruction.
    Step 3: Reread the story for fun.

AL: Suggest that the group divide into two teams, one to speak for the boys who caught the frog and the other to argue against the capture. Help the group establish simple rules to be followed during the debate. Give the children time to prepare their arguments and then to debate their side. Encourage the evaluation of each argument, helping the children to make positive comments about the performance of their own and the opposing side.

DAY 5

Creative Writing

Ask the children to write a story about a frog or other animal in the story. Discuss what is appropriate to include in the story. Help students to understand that the story needs a beginning, middle, and end. Brainstorm things known about the subject, and list them on the board for students' reference. Circulate during this activity, helping students who are unsure, reminding them to use capital letters at the beginning of sentences and encouraging the effort of all students.

For students whose writing skills are still emerging, it is appropriate to allow a group to dictate to an adult. The strengths and weaknesses of the story can then be analyzed without personal feelings becoming involved. It is unrealistic to expect mastery of mechanics from these students.

Independent Activities

Materials

    Paper for "Noun Book"

    Paper dinner plates

    Frog-shaped books for creative writing

    Frog-shaped word cards for fishing game

    Fishing pole

    Small cards, each containing one of the letters in "Christopher Columbus"

    Papers with the outline of Columbus' ship

Extension Activities

- Match rhyming words from the vocabulary in *Jump, Frog, Jump.* Students can create two-sentence rhymes using these words. With young children, this can be done orally. More mature children can write the rhymes and illustrate them.

- Sort the vocabulary words into nouns, verbs, and adjectives. Make a "Noun Book," etc. on folded paper. At this stage, it would be best to do each part of speech on a different day.

- Have each child select some of the words or phrases and illustrate them on 9-by-13-inch paper folded into fourths or in a "flap book" (see illustration on p. 19).

- Illustrate and label the life cycle of a frog on folded paper.

- Divide a paper plate into slices (4 or 6) by folding or marking them with a crayon. On each "slice," illustrate a long or short o word, noun, verb, or adjective, using the vocabulary from the book.

- Write a frog story (creative or factual) in a frog-shaped book.

Small Group and Center Activities

- Draw fish or frog shapes on construction paper cards. Write the vocabulary words on them. Put a paper clip or several staples on the end of each card. Make a fishing pole by attaching a magnet to a string and tying it to a short pole or stick. Place the word cards in a small bowl or plastic wading pool. The children must read the word on the card they catch with the magnet in order to keep it.

- Fold a piece of 12-by-8-inch manila paper into eighths. Illustrate the life cycle of an insect on the upper four boxes and the life cycle of a frog on the lower row.

- Write the letters of Christopher Columbus' name on individual cards. Place these in a container. Put papers with the outline of a ship near the container. Let the children use the letters to form new words, which they record on the outline of the ship.

- Make a ship rhyming book. Give the students the outline of a ship. They are to trace around it to make covers and pages. On page 1 at the top, they write "ship" and words that rhyme with it. Page 2 is for "boat" and its rhyming words. Continue with related words. Staple the book together.

Science

- Compare the life cycle of a frog to that of a butterfly.

- Sequence the life cycle of a frog on folded paper or on paper cut into a large circle. The circle should be divided into fourths, with one stage in each section.

- Draw a frog and label its body parts.

- Discuss and list creatures that live in a pond. Provide and read books on pond life.

- Take a class trip to a pond. Examine pond water under a microscope. The class may want to examine plants that grow in and around a pond.

Math

Materials

Lily pad or a drawing of one

Pictures of frogs (real frogs if possible)

Gummy worms

Small Group and Center Activities

- Graph pond animals according to size, color, or other attributes suggested by students.

- Compare sizes of pond animals

- Make up simple addition and subtraction stories involving pond animals. The children may do this orally; the more advanced may write the story and an equation. Example: *Five frogs were sitting on a lily pad. Two more frogs joined them. How many frogs were sitting on the lily pad in all? 5+2=7. Now there are seven frogs. Five frogs jumped back into the water. How many frogs are left? 7-5=2.*

- Measure the width of a lily pad. Measure the length. How many frogs do you think could fit on the lily pad?

- Measure the length and width of a frog with its legs extended. Now measure a frog in a sitting position. Compare.

- Find out the length of a common snake found in a pond. Mark that length on a piece of paper. Are all snakes the same length? Explain why or why not.

- Measure gummy worms. Do some comparisons with the measurements of frogs, snakes, and gummy worms. Then eat the gummy worm.

- Graph gummy worm colors.

Social Studies

Introduce literature and poetry about Christopher Columbus during the first week of October. If some children in the class are able to read this material, encourage them to read to others. Otherwise you can read aloud to the class. Initiate discussions and then follow up with extension projects.

Foreign Language

Introduce the names of some common animals found around a pond.

What is the word for "frog"? Translate the sentence "Jump, frog, jump" into the foreign language. Have the children act out the sentence.

Music

Danse Macabre by Saint-Saens

During the Halloween season, this music may be successfully combined with spooky literature, poetry, and seasonal art.

Tell the children that many years ago a French composer, Saint-Saens, composed a piece of music describing events that could take place on Halloween night. The title, *Danse Macabre,* means a dance of death.

Tell or read the story of the music. If you listen carefully, you will "hear" the story the music tells. Listen for the clock striking twelve, for Death tuning his fiddle, the rattle of bones, the ghosts dancing, and, at the end, the rooster crowing.

Play the music for the children. During this listening session, help them pick out the sounds that describe the story.

Art

Materials

18-by-9-inch construction paper, one sheet per child
(background colors: light gray, light blue, off white)

Blue construction paper for water and sky
Brown paper for ships
White construction paper for ships' sails
Assorted colors for ship, clouds, etc.

Make a mural of Columbus' ships Nina, Pinta, and Santa Maria, using cut or torn paper.

Children cut blue paper for water (encourage the use of waves) and sky for background and glue to the background paper. They cut ships and sails and glue them to the background to produce a scene of the three ships sailing on the ocean. (Show them a drawing or photo.) Children can then be motivated to write a sentence or short story about their collage.

Week 2: Overview

Instructional Books

Brown Bear, Brown Bear by Bill Martin, Jr.
Pumpkin, Pumpkin by Juan Tetherington

Related Books

The Biggest Pumpkin Ever by Steven Kroll (to be read aloud)
The Ghost Eye Tree by Bill Martin, Jr., and John Archambault (to be read aloud)
The Magic Pumpkin by Bill Martin, Jr., and John Archambault (to be read aloud)
Polar Bear, Polar Bear by Bill Martin, Jr.
Bill Martin, Jr., titles (to be read aloud)

Poems

"Magic Vine" author unknown
"12 October" by Myra Cohn Livingston
"Leaf Dance" by Rochelle Neilsen-Barsuhn

Objectives

1. **Phonetic skills**
   Review long e
   Review short e.
   Review short and long u.
   Begin to understand a vowel followed by r.
2. **Structural skills**
   Review nouns, verbs, and adjectives.
3. **Punctuation**
   Review question marks.
   Review capital letters and periods.
4. **Comprehension**
   Review the concept of cause and effect.

Materials

Word cards: pumpkin shape on orange paper

Small picture of animals in *Pumpkin, Pumpkin*

Poetry and Skills Session

DAY 1

"Leaf Dance"

Step 1: Read the poem together several times.
Step 2: Review the sound of long e as in "leaf." Ask for other words that have this sound.
Step 3: Begin a list of words that contain long e.
Step 4: Read the poem once more for enjoyment.
Step 5: Distribute copies of the poem for your students to illustrate and include in their poetry notebooks.

DAY 2

"Magic Vine"

Step 1: Before introducing the new poem, reread the poem from the previous session and review the long e sound.
Step 2: Introduce the poem and read it several times with the class. Invite children to join in as they feel comfortable.
Step 3: Discuss the "magic" of the vine.

Step 4: Mark the long and short vowels in the poem.

Step 5: Read the poem once more for pleasure.

DAY 3

"12 October"

Step 1: Read this poem and discuss the its significance.

Step 2: Encourage children to speculate on how Columbus came to the conclusion that the earth is round. Help them understand that little was known about the science of the earth at that time.

Step 3: Read the poem once more for pleasure.

DAY 4

"12 October"

Step 1: Review the vowel sounds.

Step 2: Ask the children to mark with washable markers (if the poem is laminated) the vowel sounds they know.

Step 3: Reread the poems that have been introduced this week, and use this opportunity for reteaching. A few children will have mastered the objectives. Their expertise can be useful. Ask them to help others who are having trouble.

Step 4: After a short review session, arrange the class in small groups with no more than four per group. Give each group a copy of one of the poems. Ask them to mark words with short vowel sounds. Encourage group discussions. In this way, the children who have mastered the sounds of the vowels will be able to assist those who are not yet hearing the sounds.

Step 5: After five to ten minutes, depending on the maturity of the group, reassemble the class and share the results. Do not expect mastery from all children.

DAY 5

Let the children choose poems they enjoy to read aloud, either individually or in small groups. Reading with a friend allows emerging readers to read with increasing fluency.

Reading Instruction

DAY 1

Pumpkin, Pumpkin

Shared Reading

Step 1: Introduce the book. Ask for predictions. Record these predictions on the chalkboard or chart paper.

Step 2: Begin the initial reading of the book, stopping frequently to ask what will happen next.

Step 3: If the children don't notice independently, help them observe the charming animals on each page.

Step 4: At the end of the reading, compare the actual story with the predictions. Help the children accept all suggestions; there are no wrong answers.

Step 5: From the book, choose a list of vocabulary words to be highlighted this week. If possible, let the class choose the words and write them on pumpkin shapes. Choose the number of words that equals the number of members in the class so that during cloze activities all children will be able to participate.

Small Group Instruction

Mix all ability levels to read the story for enjoyment. Before the group meets, prepare some riddles to go with small animal drawings on each page. These can be written on construction paper and laminated. Put magnetic tape on the back so they can be placed on the chalkboard (masking tape will serve the same purpose). Children are to match animal names to the riddle. Students can also make riddles for you to print on pieces of paper. Example: *I am small. I am black and red. I am an insect. I eat aphids. What am I?* (ladybug)

During this activity, emphasize "what" and the question mark. Although this is easier for the more capable children, the class can work in small groups, sharing ideas and abilities.

Invite the groups to share their riddles at the end of a work period. This is a good way to have the children use the vocabulary in the book. They can refer to the book for spelling as well as ideas. This activity is an excellent opportunity for you to circulate among the students and check comprehension skills. Make note of children who need help with a particular skill. Regroup the children for this purpose at a later time.

DAY 2

Pumpkin, Pumpkin

Shared Reading

Step 1: Reread the story. Allow time to discuss the illustrations and compare them to pictures in *Jump, Frog, Jump* and other books.

Step 2: Read the story again, looking for words that contain short u and short o.

Step 3: Review the vocabulary highlighted this week.

Small Group Instruction

EL:

Step 1: Review the vocabulary cards by placing them face up on a table.

Step 2: Allow each child to select a card, read the word, and use the word in a sentence.

Step 3: Ask each child to find that word in the text and read the sentence to the group, with assistance as needed.

Step 4: Write on the board the difficult words. Review decoding skills.

TL: Review the vocabulary. Use directed reading strategies and ask children to find sentences that answer specific questions.

AL:

Step 1: Focus on the sequence of the story. Identify cause and effect.

Step 2: Help the children outline the story by writing the events on the board and then placing them in order.

Step 3: Allow discussion on why one event must precede another. Example: Why is the seed in the child's hand before it is shown sprouting?

Day 3

Shared Reading

Step 1: Before the session begins, cover the chosen vocabulary with paper. Then distribute the words to the class. As the book is read aloud, individuals are to hold up a hidden word. Be sure that each child has an opportunity to supply a word.

Step 2: Ask the students to identify compound words in the story. Make a list of these words.

Step 3: Review nouns and verbs.

Step 4: Ask individuals to choose a page. Allow time for the children to locate the nouns and verbs on that page.

Step 5: Focus on the names of animals. Write them on cards. If possible, have pictures of these animals; otherwise, use the book. Allow time to match the names with the pictures.

Step 6: Write corresponding verbs on cards and then match them to the nouns. Examples: *mouse - creeps, grasshopper - hops* or *jumps*.

Step 7: Arrange the animal cards in alphabetical order.

Small Group Instruction

Step 1: Mix ability groups. Choose a child to be IT.

Step 2: The child turns away from the group; someone places a vocabulary card on the board.

Step 3: Without using the actual word, children in the group offer clues to the word's meaning.

Step 4: IT tries to guess the word. If the child guesses the word after three clues, the child who gave the clues is the next IT.

Note: Before playing this game for the first time, discuss with children what good clues are and how to go about giving good descriptions in three clues.

DAY 4

Brown Bear, Brown Bear

Shared Reading

Step 1: Read the following biographical sketch of Bill Martin, Jr.

Biographical Sketch of Bill Martin, Jr.

William Ivan Martin has touched the lives of children in many ways. He has been a teacher, a principal, and a storyteller; written language textbooks; and, of course, written books for children (Commire 1977). One of the people with whom he frequently works is Eric Carle.

Mr. Martin was born in Kansas in 1916. He loved listening to his grandmother tell him stories about being a pioneer on the Oklahoma prairie. He learned that it is important to memorize stories and songs that you like because in that way you will always have them with you.

He liked to dream when he was small, and he could go anywhere and do anything in his imagination. He was in his twenties before he began putting his dreams on paper (Author Profile, SeeSaw 1990).

Mr. Martin has three college degrees and enjoys meeting with children and talking to them about the books they like to read. He often includes music in these visits. His books use interesting words and rhythms that invoke musical feelings when read (Rudin 1990).

Mr. Martin moved from New York City to the quiet of Campbell, Texas, in 1993. He now lives in the woods and enjoys watching the animals around his house. He relates that many of his ideas come from his observation of animals, and often something someone says may give him an idea for a new book. His favorite book is the one on which he is currently working. He continues to work with Eric Carle, John Archambault, and others through the technology of fax machines and the telephone (Bryant 1993).

Step 2: Introduce the book. Ask for predictions.

Step 3: Read together with emphasis on fluency and rhythm.

Step 4: Read the book again, sequencing the names of animals on the board as they appear in the story. As an additional activity, sequence strips of color as they appear in the story.

Step 5: Discuss the sound of short e. Find words in the book that have this sound. This is one of the most difficult short vowels to hear because of differences in dialect, so help the children accept that there is a "pure" way to say it, as heard in "pen" as opposed to "pin." It may be difficult for them to hear the difference. For the children who have mastered the short e, move on to another skill, such as e followed by r, as in her.

Small Group Instruction

EL: Allow the children to retell the story, using word cards that contain the names and colors of the animals. Discuss which of the colors are real and which are fictional.

TL:

Step 1: Sequence animals and colors.

Step 2: Discuss real and make-believe.

Step 3: Place words in groups according to nouns and adjectives.

Step 4: Allow each child to take the part of an animal and read the story in sequence.

AL: Encourage this group to write another version of the story by suggesting a theme (for example, animals) that would be appropriate. The purpose of this is to stimulate some creative thought in the group.

Accept all answers. Keep in mind that even the silliest ideas may trigger an exceptional response in other children. This method of "piggy-backing" is an accepted part of brainstorming.

DAY 5

Brown Bear

Shared Reading

Step 1: Reread the story for fun.

Step 2: Encourage the class to add to the story. Ask what other animals could be seen. What might follow?

Step 3: Ask one child to be IT, and begin a story with an original idea. To help begin the process, you can model by saying, "Smelly skunk, smelly skunk, what do you see?" Another child can then become the skunk and respond, "I see a _____ looking at me." Involve as many of the children as time allows.

Distribute paper that has been folded into small books. Let the children write their own version of the story. While they are working independently, you are free to offer individual help.

Although the objective is to help children write with ease and fluency, reminders can be given about beginning sentences with capital letters. Young children who are not comfortable with extended writing activities can use pictures to tell the stories, and you can help with the writing.

Independent Activities

Materials

Small books, one per child, for creative writing (perhaps in seasonal shapes)

12-by-18-inch drawing paper

Large plastic pumpkin

Pictures on small cards, to be used in a vowel game

Cards with vowels written on them

Assortment of small paper pumpkins with nouns, verbs, and adjectives written on them

Cards with pictures of animals

Cards with matching names of animals

Extension Activities

- Rewrite *Brown Bear*, and make individual books. These can be made in a seasonal-shaped accordion book (for example, pumpkin, witch, or cat) or in a design of the children's choosing. See the directions for shaped accordion books on page 23.

- Write and illustrate adjectives in pumpkin-shaped books.

- Make vowel books. Draw a Halloween shape (for example, pumpkin, witch's hat, cat, or ghost) on paper. Make copies available to the children. They are to write a vowel at the top of the page and list words with that sound. They will need a page for each vowel included. This is a good tool for evaluation.

- Write a sequence story: "How Jamie Grew a Pumpkin."

- Reproduce animal riddles written by the children. Each child reads the riddle, answers it, cuts it out following predrawn lines, and glues it into a section on a piece of 12-by-8-inch paper folded into fourths. Using both sides of the paper, eight riddles can be used. The sections can be cut following the folded lines and stapled together into a riddle book. Have the children design a cover and take the book home to share the riddles and their increasing reading abilities.

Small Group and Center Activities

- Purchase a large plastic pumpkin. These should be available in Halloween displays. Write vocabulary words on small pumpkin shapes and place them in the large container. Have the children take turns pulling a word from the pumpkin. If they identify the word correctly, they can keep it. Otherwise, it goes back into the pumpkin. The game continues until all words are used.

- A variation of this game is to paste small pictures on orange cards, which are arranged face up on the floor. Write vowels on word cards and place them inside the pumpkin. As a vowel is drawn, it is matched to a picture. Include more vowels than pictures to make this more challenging.

- Another variation is to write nouns, verbs, or adjectives on the small pumpkins. The words can be sorted by category or read and used in a sentence.

- A matching game can be made by pasting riddles and the names of animals on cards. The children match an animal to a riddle.

Science

Materials

Pumpkin

Knife for carving

Spoon

Paper cups or empty milk cartons

- Cut a pumpkin and scoop out the seeds. Examine the pulp and seeds under a microscope. Clean some of the seeds and plant them in individual containers. Paper cups or half-pint milk cartons (with the tops removed) work well. Record growth stages on a chart, on a graph, or in a "pumpkin journal."

- On a folded piece of paper, illustrate and label the growing cycle of a pumpkin as presented in *Pumpkin, Pumpkin*. List ways to use pumpkins.

- Help the children do some research on real bears by reading some factual books on bears. Compare and contrast with *Brown Bear* and *Polar Bear*. Write a class story. Make individual copies for the children to read and illustrate.

Math

Materials

Teddy bear counters

Orange construction paper

Box of sand

Bear shapes

- Children can manipulate pumpkin seeds into sets for simple addition and subtraction practice. Ask them to make up number stories for the others to solve with their pumpkin seeds. Some of the children may want to write number sentences on their slates or on paper. Pumpkin seeds can be purchased, or raw ones can be cooked ahead of time. The children can eat their work at the end of the session.

- Plastic teddy bear counters (available in plastic tubs from manipulative math supply catalogs) can be used in the same way as the pumpkin seeds. Encourage children to write their stories on paper, exchange them with a partner, and solve them. The number stories can also be bound into a class big book for the children to solve during free time, either individually or with a partner.

- Cut pumpkins from orange construction paper. Use math facts being studied. Write a fact on one pumpkin and the answer on another. The children then match the pumpkins. These can be used on the board if magnetic tape is attached to the back. Alternatively, a box of sand can make a "bed" and the "fact pumpkins" can be made to stand in rows under the answer.

- The preceding activity can also be used with bear shapes. The facts can be on polar bears and the answers on brown bears.

Music

Continue with *Danse Macabre*. During this week, teach the children that a composer must use various appropriate sounds to tell a musical story. Have a selection of rhythm instruments available. (We are assuming that the children are familiar with the instruments and the sounds they make.)

Ask the children to agree on an instrument that sounds like the clock striking twelve. Guide them through a selection of instruments and sounds that describe what is happening in the story. Retell or read the story again, encouraging the children to add their sounds at the appropriate place in the story. Repeat this activity several times during the month, giving all children an opportunity to sound an instrument.

Art

Materials

Drawing paper

Watercolors

Orange construction paper

- As a follow-up to the music activity, the children can draw with crayons or paint their own impressions of the bear's trip over the mountain.

- A lesson on folding paper and cutting a freehand pumpkin can follow the reading of *Pumpkin, Pumpkin*. The children then decorate their own jack-o-lanterns with crayons or paint. For more skilled children, the eyes, nose, and mouth can be cut out and then a piece of yellow construction paper pasted on the back to resemble the candlelight showing through. This is an excellent opportunity to discuss circles, triangles, and squares.

Week 3: Overview

Instructional Books

Nobody by Pat Edwards
Red Leaf, Yellow Leaf by Lois Ehlert
Leaves by June Epstein
The Witches' Little Sister by JoAnne Nelson
A Tree Is Nice by Janice Undry

Related Titles

A Dark, Dark Tale by Ruth Brown (to be read aloud)
Scary, Scary Halloween by Eve Bunting (to be read aloud)

Good-Night, Owl! by Pat Hutchins (to be read aloud)
Witch, Witch, Come to My Party by Arden Druce (to be read aloud)
Barn Dance by Bill Martin, Jr., and John Archambault (to be read aloud)
Other titles by Bill Martin, Jr., (to be read aloud)
A Chair for My Mother by Vera B. Williams (to be read aloud)
Other titles by Vera B. Williams (to be read aloud)

Poems

"Hello Halloween" author unknown
"Down, Down" by Eleanor Farjean
"Fall Hills" by Janae Belk Moncure

Music

Pines of Rome by Respighi

Objectives

1. **Phonetic skills**
   Review short and long e, o, and u.
   Begin to understand ow and ou.
2. **Structural skills**
   Begin to understand the concept of root words and endings.
   Review compound words.
3. **Punctuation**
   Review capitals, periods, and question marks.
   Review apostrophe.
4. **Alphabetical sequence**
   Review alphabetical order.

Materials

Sentence strips

Word cards in the shape of a witch's hat

Word cards in the shape of ghosts

Poetry and Skills Session

If these poems are not available, any Halloween poetry can be substituted.

DAY 1

"Hello Halloween"

Step 1: Read the poem together.

Step 2: Have the children discuss it and add their own ideas of what excites them about this holiday.

Step 3: Review short and long e. Find words in the poem that contain these vowels.

Step 4: Review short and long o. Identify words in the poem that contain these vowels.

Step 5: Read the poem again for enjoyment.

Step 6: Distribute copies of the poem for your students to illustrate and include in their poetry notebooks.

DAY 2

"Fall Hills"

Step 1: Read together and discuss the content. The children may comment on the form of the poem: the first, third, and fifth lines begin with capital letters, while the other lines in the poem are indented and begin with lowercase letters. It is appropriate for students to begin noticing such things in poetry. They need to understand that the rules for writing prose do not have to be followed in poetry.

Step 2: Point out that "Halloween" begins with a capital letter because it is the name of a holiday.

DAY 3

"Down, Down"

Step 1: Read the poem several times for enjoyment.

Step 2: Review long and short o.

Step 3: Introduce ow. Ask children if they can think of other words that have this sound.

Step 4: Explain that ou can make the same sound as ow. Give example words, such as "sound," "found," and "round." Write these words on a chart for later use.

Step 5: Read the poem again for fun.

DAY 4

"Down, Down"

Step 1: Reread and discuss the poem briefly.

Step 2: Review the sounds from the previous lesson.

Step 3: Go over the list of words from the previous session that contain ou and ow. Do not expect reading mastery at this time.

DAY 5

Read from poetry books for pleasure.

Reading Instruction

DAY 1

The Witches' Little Sister

Shared Reading

Step 1: Introduce the book to the class.

Step 2: Ask for predictions about the story. Record these on the chalkboard or large chart paper. Ask the children to listen to the story to discover what problems the little witch has and how she solves them.

Step 3: Read the story, allowing time for student comments.

Step 4: Discuss the little witch's problems, and then reread the story, inviting the children to join in.

Small Group Instruction

Mix children of varying abilities for this session. Read the story together. Allow time for comments about the illustrations.

DAY 2

The Witches' Little Sister

Shared Reading

Step 1: Reread the story, encouraging children to join in as the story is read.

Step 2: Write vocabulary words or phrases on sentence strip paper. Pass these out to the children.

Step 3: After each child reads a word or phrase, ask him or her to match it to the text in the book. The group then reads the sentence that contains this word or phrase.

Small Group Instruction

EL:

Step 1: Distribute copies of *Nobody* to the group and read it together. The children enjoy the format of this book and will enjoy the humor in it.

Step 2: Identify vocabulary that presents problems. Write the words on cards or ghost-shaped paper.

Step 3: Review the concept of compound words. Examples: *bathroom, bedroom*.

Step 4: Reteach the apostrophe as used in contractions.

TL:

Step 1: Read *The Witches' Little Sister*.

Step 2: Use this session to help the children master difficult vocabulary. Identify the difficult words and make word cards for them. Play some vocabulary games that will help the students remember the words.

Step 3: Read at least part of the book together. Do not become so focused on what these children need to learn that the joy of the story is lost.

AL:

Step 1: Have the students read *The Witches' Little Sister* silently; you can assist with vocabulary as needed.

Step 2: Discuss the reason for meeting on the 21st of June (first day of summer), and relate this to Halloween.

Step 3: Ask for suggestions about things witches might do when they get together and the problems they might face. This discussion will be a foundation for later sessions with this group.

DAY 3

The Witches' Little Sister

Shared Reading

Step 1: Divide the children into two groups. Reread the story in unison.

Step 2: Little Witch has trouble remembering what is needed. Discuss what is forgotten and how it relates to the trip.

Step 3: Encourage the children to suggest ways for Little Witch to remember the things she needs.

Small Group Instruction

EL:

Step 1: Play a vocabulary game with words from *Nobody*. Let each child choose a word, read it, and use it in a sentence. This activity will help the students learn the vocabulary.

Step 2: Identify nouns, verbs, and adjectives, and place words in alphabetical order.

Step 3: Read the story, letting some of the group read the girl's part and others that of the ghost.

TL:

Step 1: Spread the vocabulary words from *The Witches' Little Sister* on the reading table. Ask each child to choose a word, read it, and use it in a sentence.

Step 2: Ask volunteers to place the words in alphabetical order.

Step 3: Reread the story by having each child choose a favorite page to read aloud. This helps identify those who are having trouble with certain words.

AL:

Step 1: Ask the group to discuss the reality of witches. Lead the children to conclude that they are fictional and that in literature witches have a bad reputation.

Step 2: Have the students list stories that have witches in them, identifying the kind of character witches usually play.

Step 3: Suggest that it is time to change the reputation of witches. Ask this group how they could help people become more sympathetic toward witches. Encourage them to formulate a plan that will change the common view. One idea might be an advertising campaign that would alter preconceived ideas. The group could make posters to "sell" the idea that witches should be treated fairly.

In some communities, there may be a concern about an activity related to witches. Be sensitive to opinions of parents on this issue. If the idea of witches is not acceptable, the subject could be black cats or any other superstition. It is important that this project be undertaken in a spirit of fun.

DAY 4

Shared Reading

- During this session, have the children brainstorm a list of Halloween words and write them on chart paper. Provide small pieces of paper on which the children can illustrate the words they suggest. Then they are to paste the illustrations on the chart beside the words. This creates a picture dictionary of Halloween words that the entire class can see, read, and use in writing activities.

- Introduce root words and endings.
- An optional activity might be to have the children copy the words in a small student-made book for their own dictionary of Halloween words.

Small Group Instruction

EL:

Step 1: Continue working with the vocabulary from *Nobody*. Focus on skills presented in shared reading sessions, and use this time for reteaching.

Step 2: Review root words and endings. Identify from the story a word that has an ending.

Step 3: Help the children locate words with the vowel sounds discussed. Always let them volunteer rather than putting someone on the spot. If a child has particular trouble, ask him or her to select a word and identify the vowel sound in that word. Children having difficulty can thus gain confidence.

Step 4: Read the story aloud as a group.

TL:

Step 1: Follow a procedure similar to that of the first group. Using *The Witches' Little Sister,* work on the vocabulary and review phonetic skills. Use this time to address any individual needs children in the group may have.

Step 2: Let the children choose a partner from the group and read the story with the partner.

AL: Continue with the campaign to change the image of witches as portrayed in literature. Encourage creative ideas. If others in the class wish to join in, allow them to participate.

Suggest that the children debate the issue. Have half of the group advocate the inclusion of witch characters in stories, with the other half taking the opposite side. It is your role as debate judge to decide what is an appropriate argument, thereby keeping the participation under control.

DAY 5

Shared Reading

Step 1: Help the children retell the story of the Little Witch.

Step 2: Name all of the things the Little Witch forgot and all of the places she had to go to find them.

Step 3: Categorize the words according to nouns (naming words), verbs (doing words), and adjectives (describing words).

Step 4: Cover the words "witches" and "riding" in the text. Have the children suggest words that could be substituted for witches in the first line and an action word to use in place of "riding" in the third. List suggestions on the board.

Step 5: Show the children how new words can be inserted in the pattern of the story and give them time to enjoy reading the new text together. Example:

The *black bats* had a meeting
on the 21st of June,
and decided they'd go *flying*
in and out around the moon.

Depending upon the group, this activity can proceed to more complete rewriting, such as the following:

The children had a hayride
on Halloween Day,
and decided they'd go riding
in a wagon full of hay.

This activity involves a lot of time. After the whole group chooses some examples, break into small groups and ask the children to write more rhymes. Print at least one "poem" from each group on large paper and make a class big book of the poems. If children are able, they can work in pairs to write the entries.

Independent activities

Materials

Orange construction paper and manila paper stapled together to make books

Phrases from *The Witches' Little Sister* duplicated for use by emergent writers

Black construction paper and writing paper

Paper lunch sacks for puppets

Word cards, cut and colored to look like seed packets

Extension Activities

- Have the children write a creative version of *Brown Bear* called "Orange Pumpkin, Orange Pumpkin." Cut pumpkin shapes from 12-by-18-inch orange paper for the covers, and use manila paper for the leaves. Staple the pages together to form a blank book. Instruct the children to use Halloween words from the Halloween word list and/or picture dictionary and include color words in the story.

The objective is to have each sentence contain a noun and an adjective. Follow the rhyme of *Brown Bear* by beginning "Orange Pumpkin, Orange Pumpkin, what do you see? I see a black cat looking at me. Black Cat, Black Cat, what do you see?" and so on. It is appropriate to do at least two pages with the children to help them understand the format. As the book continues, some children may want to change the adjective from color words to "scary," "ugly," and so on. When the book is complete, help the children write a title page. They may wish to include a dedication also.

This activity may take up to a week to complete, but it is a delightful creative project to read and reread. The book offers an excellent opportunity to share writing activities with other children. Encourage the children to read their books to a kindergarten class or, for shy children, to one or two younger students.

Ask the children to illustrate each page, perhaps including borders on the pages. Books by Vera B. Williams are excellent models for the use of borders. Some of Ms. Williams books that work well for this activity are as follows:

A Chair for My Mother
Cherries and Cherry Pits
Music, Music for Everyone

- Construct a large book shaped like a witch's hat, with blank pages for each child. After reading *Witch, Witch, Come to My Party* once or twice to the class, suggest that children write their own books inviting Halloween characters to a party. Example: "Skeleton, Skeleton, please come to my party." Second page: "Thank you, I will if you invite Bat." Third page: "Bat, Bat, please come to my party." Fourth page: "Thank you, I will if you invite Goblin."

- This activity provides opportunity for illustrations that encourage creative expression, and it lets children make use of their Halloween dictionaries.

- Some young children are not ready for long writing activities this early in the year. To help them succeed with this activity, provide a "secretary" to whom they can dictate their story and then do their own illustrations. This "secretary" could be an older student or a parent volunteer.

- Select phrases from *The Witches' Little Sister* (for example, "The witches decided to have a meeting"). Write the phrases on paper, enclosing each in a box so the lines can be used as a cutting guide. Make copies for the children. The children cut these out, place them on folded paper or a "flip-book," and illustrate them. These can be used to evaluate comprehension.

- Create ghost stories based on *Nobody*. First staple handwriting paper between two sheets of black paper. Then paste a pocket on the front. Each child is to create a ghost to hide in the pocket on the cover.

Small Group and Center Activities

- Play "Concentration," using vocabulary words from any of the books.

- Have the children make puppets to act out one of the Halloween stories. Provide paper lunch sacks and scraps of construction paper. (Have a large cardboard box in a convenient location. Teach the children to put reusable scraps of paper in it, to be used for other projects.) When the play is complete, the students act it out for another class.

- Put Halloween words on cards that look like seed packets. Glue these to craft sticks. Provide a box with two inches of sand in the bottom. The children plant the words in alphabetical order.

Science

Materials

Samples of simple and compound leaves, glued to tag board and laminated

Cards with samples of leaves glued to them and laminated

Outline of large tree for use on a bulletin board

If possible, provide a copy of *Leaves* for each child. If individual copies are not available, allow the children to share or look at your copy. Read the book in an instructional, rather than recreational, manner. Lead the children in the following activities:

- Discuss the changing color of leaves in the fall, pointing out that during the summer, the green leaves are manufacturing food for the tree with the help of the sun ("photosynthesis"). Use this term with the children, but do not expect all of them to remember it. However, through frequent use of the term during discussions, some children will master the word and the meaning.

- Gather examples of simple and compound leaves. Help children discover the difference between the two. Gather examples of smooth, toothed, and lobed leaves. Glue them to a large piece of tag board, label them, laminate the chart, and hang it in the classroom for use as a reference tool.

- Cut tag board or other firm paper into 6-inch squares. Glue examples of the types of leaves to the squares, one leaf to a square. You will need several examples of each. Laminate the squares. The children can use these for sorting and classifying activities.

Note: When laminated, these examples will last indefinitely.

- Compare examples of toothed, lobed, and smooth-edged leaves with needles from evergreens.

- Make a leaf booklet or decorative pictures by using the laminated leaves to do leaf rubbings. The rubbings should be labeled "simple" or "compound" and identified as examples of smooth, toothed, or lobed leaves.

- Discuss things that are made from trees. What grows on trees? Individual or class books can be assembled from illustrations made by the children. This is also appropriate for a bulletin board. The children can add to the board as new items are discovered. This ongoing activity will develop an awareness of the place of trees in our environment, and students will become aware of the need for conservation.

- In the book *Leaves,* children learn how a tree grows from a seed. After a tree sprouts leaves, the bud form for the next year can be seen. Look at branches and identify the leaf bud. Draw the life cycle of a tree. The children then compare this to the life cycle of a pumpkin.

- Read *A Tree Is Nice* to the class. Direct the children to illustrate the four seasons on a 12-by-8-inch sheet of paper folded into fourths. Encourage them to include the appropriate background and write a short sentence at the bottom of each picture. If they are not ready to write a sentence, they can just label each section with the name of the season.

- Read *Good-Night, Owl!* to the class. Discuss the animals that live in and around trees. Books, booklets, or pictures can be made, illustrating the animals and their homes.

- Discuss why cutting down forest land is destructive to these animals and to the ecology of the earth. This is a good cooperative activity, letting the children work in groups of two or three.

- Put a large tree on a bulletin board. Ask the students to draw, color, and cut out the animals from *Good-Night, Owl!* and put them on the tree. This can also be done individually on 12-by-18-inch paper. When children draw a background and then cut out pictures to add to it, the final product has a collage appearance rather than that of a simple drawing.

Math

Step 1: Discuss the attributes of leaves gathered during this week: size, shape, texture, and color.

Step 2: Graph leaves according to size, color, or particular kind, such as maple, oak, etc.

Step 3: Using the leaves, encourage children to create story problems. They can work with a partner and take turns writing number sentences on their slates or on leaves cut from paper.

Social Studies

Look at a map of the United States. Find the approximate location of your hometown. Discuss the changes that occur in fall in your state. Compare and contrast the changes to those of fall in other states. Depending upon the experience of the class, discuss how early the effects of the change of season are observable. Example: Maine experiences cool weather earlier than does Texas.

This experience with maps will begin to build a foundation for the social studies work in November and December. Do not expect mastery of state names. Use this as a pre-assessment time to determine what the children know about maps.

Foreign Language

Play a recording of "Autumn Leaves" in the foreign language your class is studying. Introduce the foreign words for *trees, leaves, fall, color,* and *ground.*

Music

After the children have become familiar with *Danse Macabre,* suggest that they sound their instruments while listening to the music without the benefit of the narrative. For this to be successful, the children must be familiar with both the music and the story.

Art

Materials

Construction paper in brown and autumn colors

Tempera paint in autumn colors

Sponge

Watercolors

- After reading *A Tree Is Nice,* ask the children to create a fall tree by using one of the following media:

  Cut a bare tree from brown construction paper. Glue the tree to a neutral background. Tear colored leaves from construction paper scraps and paste them on and around the bare tree to create a fall tree. Don't forget colored leaves at the bottom of the tree to jump in!

  Using the same method of constructing a tree on a neutral background, add the leaves with pieces of sponge dipped in tempera paint.

- Have the children paint one side of a blank piece of paper with watercolors, making sure the whole side is covered. Encourage them to paint in a rainbow, using the colors of fall leaves. After the painted sheet is absolutely dry, reverse the paper and trace different kinds of leaves on the blank side. Label and cut out the leaves. Use these colorful leaves for collages, bulletin board trees, or mobiles. They can also be used to create leaf people.

Week 4: Overview

Instructional Books

Teeny Tiny by Jill Bennett
Henny Penny by H. Werner Zimmerman

Related Titles

Wobble the Witch Cat by Mary Calhoun (to be read aloud)
Cranberry Halloween by Wende and Harry Devlin (to be read aloud)

The Witch Who Was Afraid of Witches by Alice Low (to be read aloud)
Hildilid's Night by Cheli Duran Ryan (to be read aloud)
Little Old Lady Who Was Not Afraid of Anything by Linda Williams (to be read aloud)
In a Scary Old House by Harriet Ziefect (to be read aloud)

Poems

"My Brother" by Dorothy Aldis
"The Goblin" by Rose Fyleman
"Skeleton Parade" by Jack Prelutsky

Objectives

1. **Phonetic skills**
   Review long and short vowels previously introduced.
2. **Structural analysis**
   Review nouns, verbs, and adjectives.
   Review the concept of root words and endings.
   Begin to understand the concept of compound words.
3. **Punctuation**
   Review the use of periods and question marks.
   Begin to understand the uses of quotation marks.
4. **Comprehension**
   Review the concepts of fact and fiction.
   Begin to understand the concept of main idea.

Materials

Word cards in the shape of a pot, similar to the one Henny Penny wears

Word cards in the shape of bones

Poetry and Skills Session

DAY 1

"Skeleton Parade"

Step 1: Ask the children to close their eyes and listen to the poem. Read it twice in this manner.

Step 2: Encourage individuals to describe what they saw as they listened. The poem evokes vivid images.

Step 3: Read the poem again, encouraging student participation. The children will probably begin to move with the rhythm of the words. Allow them to get up and march around the room as it is read.

DAY 2

"Skeleton Parade"

Read the poem again, allowing time to enjoy the poem. Let volunteers mark vowels, using wipe-off markers.

DAY 3

"The Goblin"

This is another poem with an appealing rhythm. Read it twice so the children can become familiar with it. They will begin to join in during the second reading. Compare it with "Skeleton Parade," and discuss the differences. Focus briefly on the fact and fiction aspects of both poems.

DAY 4

"My Brother"

This is an excellent poem for this time of year because the children can talk about the way costumes change the appearance of people they know. Some children may still be uneasy about Halloween, and this is an opportunity for them to share their fears. If time allows, review the skills introduced during this month. This is an opportunity to identify students who need extra help.

DAY 5

Read the poems for pleasure, allowing each student to choose a favorite. If some wish to read with a partner, accept this because it is a way for emergent readers to feel comfortable while participating.

Reading Instruction

DAY 1

Henny Penny

Shared Reading

Step 1: Display the cover of the story, using the big book if it is available. Ask the children to predict what the book will be about. Record their predictions on a chalkboard.

Step 2: Read the entire book to the children, stopping frequently to discuss the charming and humorous illustrations.

Step 3: Ask for words that contain long and short o, i, e, and u.

Step 4: Help children identify this story as a fairy tale.

Small Group Instruction

Step 1: Mix all abilities during this session. Read the story together. It can be read with two children taking the role of one animal or in any way that involves all of the students.

Step 2: Write selected vocabulary on word cards. These cards can be in the shape of the pot Henny Penny wears on her head.

Step 3: Spend a few minutes with each group, discussing the target vocabulary, giving them clues for decoding the words, and identifying the sequence of the story.

DAY 2

Henny Penny

Shared Reading

Step 1: Reread the story.

Step 2: Discuss the parts of the story that are fact and those that are purely fiction.

Step 3: Ask the children to find nouns, verbs, and adjectives in the story.

Small Group Instruction

EL:

- Begin the group with a game to help children learn the vocabulary words. They can choose a word, read it, and use it in a sentence. Turn all of the cards face down on the table. As a card is drawn, the student either reads and keeps it or returns it to the pool. Children can ask a friend to help them with the word, thus allowing them to "keep" it. Don't encourage a count of words at the end to see who won. Instead emphasize that the group was able to read all of the words by working together.

- Explain the use of quotation marks in the text. Ask individuals to read sentences actually spoken by a character. Print some of these on the board and then ask children to place the quotation marks in the appropriate places.

TL:

- Read the story as a play. Each child assumes a role, with one acting as the narrator. While the story is being read, make note of the words that are giving readers trouble. At the conclusion of the session, help students use decoding clues to figure out the words.

- Go over any of the skills presented in the whole-group sessions that appear to be troublesome to the students.

AL:

- Read the story as a play. Ask the children to identify the silliest parts of the story. Answers will vary. Encourage them to explain why they think that part is so unbelievable. These points may come from the text or their interpretation of the story.

- Focus on the quotation and question marks. Ask the children to give an example of a sentence that uses quotation marks. Help them differentiate between asking and telling sentences.

DAY 3

Henny Penny

Shared Reading

Step 1: Before reading the story today, ask the children what the main events were. Write these phrases on sentence strips. Encourage discussion about which could be identified as main events.

Step 2: After the group is satisfied with the choices, ask the children to put them in order.

Step 3: Read the story, explaining that you are going to be looking for quotation marks, which can also be called "talking marks." As a page is turned, ask someone to read the part in quotation marks. Be sure that they understand the reason for these marks.

Small Group Instruction

EL: Allow this group to read the book as a play. They can help each other with words, or you can offer this support. They will know the story well enough by now that this can be done with success.

TL and AL:

- Review compound words. Ask the children to look through the book and locate compound words. List them on chart paper to keep for the children to use when they are writing their own stories.

- Explore the suffix "ing." On chart paper, make a list of verbs in the story as children find them. As they read a word, print the "ing" form beside it. Select volunteers to underline the root word and circle the ending.

- Discuss values with the class. This story encourages us to think for ourselves rather than letting another person make decisions. A poem that reinforces this concept is "Jelly Beans up Your Nose" in *The Butterfly Jar* by Jeff Moss.

DAY 4

Teeny Tiny

Shared Reading

This book is a good selection for Halloween because of the spooky element that appeals so to children. Its repetitive text makes it an appropriate choice for reading early in the year.

Step 1: Display the cover. Ask for predictions about the story. Record these predictions.

Step 2: Read the story. If no one notices the little ghost peeking at the woman on each page, guide the children's attention to it and ask why they think the ghost is always there.

Small Group Instruction

Mix the groups for the activities today. Using bones cut from construction paper ahead of time, write a vocabulary word on each. Use these for vocabulary games such as one of the following: make a sentence with each word, think of a rhyming word, arrange the words in alphabetical order, or categorize according to nouns, verbs, and adjectives.

DAY 5

Henny Penny

Shared Reading

Reread the story together. Ask for volunteers to change some part of the story and retell that part.

EL: Depending upon the assessment of this group, use either *Henny Penny* or *Teeny Tiny* for the day's activities.

Step 1: Look at the word cards from the story. Select those that have vowel sounds that you suggest.

Step 2: Sort the words into nouns, verbs, and adjectives.

Step 3: Choose a word and find a sentence in the story that contains the word. Read the sentence to the group.

TL and AL: Work with the vocabulary words from *Teeny Tiny* as did the first group.

Step 1: Focus the discussion upon the woman's feelings. Read that part of the text with appropriate expression. Encourage expansion of vocabulary to describe emotions beyond the typical *happy, sad,* or *scared.* Spend time with the last page; it offers great potential for the expression of feelings.

Step 2: To strengthen sequencing skills, have the children work in small groups and draw pictures of the important things that happen in the story. Mix abilities for this activity so that the children can help each other with writing and spelling. Students should write a brief sentence at the bottom of each picture.

Step 3: Let each group share its story with the class. Because there may be differences in opinions of what is important, allow time for discussion. Ask students to give reasons for their decisions. This activity is an excellent reinforcement for vocabulary as well as an opportunity for the assessment of comprehension.

Independent Activities

Materials

Paper plates for making puppets

Large paper for murals

Shape books for creative writing and independent activities

Shelf paper and rollers for making a "movie"

Cards with root words and cards with endings for matching game

Cards with words that can be combined to make compound words

Halloween words written on pumpkin shapes

Extension Activities

- Have children create puppets for their puppet show (*Henny Penny* or *Teeny Tiny*). Give each child a large, flat paper plate to use as the face and/or body of the puppet. Motivate the children to recreate the unusual headgear worn by the characters. They can build their puppets by taping them to 12-inch rulers, paint-stirring sticks (available at most paint stores), or empty paper towel rolls. The children hold the handles to move the puppets about. Other children can make scenery with paint, markers, or crayons. Still others can build a puppet stage from a large packing box. If a drama teacher is available, perhaps help can be enlisted.

- Read other versions of *Henny Penny* to the children or with them. Encourage the children to do comparison activities. How are the stories alike? How are they different? Fold a large piece of paper in fourths. Label the top of each half with the name of the version being compared. Depending on the abilities of the children, ask them to either write or draw ways the stories are alike and different. Use one square on each half for *same* and one for *different*.

- Select the favorite version of *Henny Penny*. Cooperative groups can create murals of their favorite. This project can continue for several days. Shelf paper is convenient for this project. Display completed murals around the room and along the halls of the school.

- Write and illustrate a class big book version of the story, or write individual versions of the story on large acorn-shaped books. Some children may want to rewrite the ending, making it a happier one.

- Make flip books, using a compound word and its parts on the front page and illustrating the word on the second page (see diagram on page 19). This activity may be adapted to root words and endings from the story, vocabulary words, parts of speech, or vowels.

- On large ghost- or bone-shaped books, write creative stories based on *Teeny Tiny*. Rewrite the ending.

- Cooperative groups can make murals of *Teeny Tiny*. If shelf paper is used, a mural can be shown as a "movie." Cut a square from the bottom of a large box. Attach the ends of the story to empty paper towel rollers. As the story is told, the "film" is rolled inside the box so it appears in the "screen."

- Write long o words on cut-out bones or ghosts. These can easily be drawn on a paper and then copied so that each child can write words on them. Children can play cooperative games with their collection of words.

Small Group and Center Activities

- The bones you made for vocabulary activities can be placed at the language center so that children can replay all of the games with a partner or in a small group.

- Write root words on sentence strip paper. Write "ing" endings on another. Children are to match root words with endings.

- In a center, locate the compound word cards you made for the children to take apart. They write on small cards the words that make the compound word. They can also write this on a sheet of paper as a math equation. Example: cup + board = cupboard.

- Have each child make a Halloween vowel book. Let the children choose a shape, use five blank pages, and write a vowel at the top of each page. A long vowel can be on one side with the short vowel on the reverse. Words are added to the pages over a period of several days.

- Write math combinations on bones or acorns. Children are to match the fact with the correct answer. Store these in an appealing container such as a plastic skull, pumpkin shell, or trick-or-treat bag.

- Write Halloween words on pumpkins or witch hats to be arranged in alphabetical order. Store these in a "creative" container.

Science

Step 1: The children should be able to recognize an oak tree and an oak leaf from their ongoing study of leaves. Review this information, and then take the class for a walk to gather acorns. If the school is not located in an area where this is possible, ask children to bring these materials to class. Other common trees can be substituted if there are no oak trees in the community.

Step 2: Discuss the fact that acorns are food for squirrels during the winter. Then save the acorns to put out for these animals during the cold days.

Step 3: The hunt for acorns can lead to a study of the types of trees that produce nuts. If time allows, use this as a motivation for exploring how animals prepare for winter.

Math

- Number stories can be based on the text of *Henny Penny*. Example: *Henny Penny, Cocky Locky, and Ducky Lucky were going to see the king. Goosey Loosey asked, "May I go with you?" How many animals were going to see the king?* 3+1=4

- Children can manipulate their real acorns to solve problems. If real acorns are not available, substitute paper ones. Ten is a sufficient number per child. Children arrange ten acorns in a row. A child can suggest, "find the fifth acorn," "divide your acorns in half," or "make three equal piles." Ask what they discovered. You can direct the activities, or the class can work in pairs.

Social Studies

Young children often have disagreements because of a misunderstanding. A discussion about how these develop can be an appropriate follow-up to *Henny Penny*. This might be the foundation for class discussions on kindness to others and the importance of thinking through a situation before taking action. Because many children need constant reminders to think for themselves when distinguishing between right and wrong, this story is an excellent springboard for ongoing discussion. If Henny Penny's friends hadn't all been followers, perhaps the story would have had a happier ending!

Foreign Language

This week the children should work with names of animals in the target language. They can also hear how the sounds of animals are made in this language. Pictures are an excellent tool for this purpose. If the animals from *Henny Penny* are used, it ties these two subjects together very nicely.

Music

During this week, play *Danse Macabre* and encourage the children to create their own stories. They can change the use of the instruments to apply to the new versions.

Art

Materials

Black and white construction paper

After reading the poem "Skeleton Parade," have each child create a skeleton from strips of white paper. The skeleton is cut and glued vertically to a sheet of 6-by-18-inch black construction paper. Each child is given a copy of "Skeleton Parade" to glue on the reverse side.

For first graders, you will have to cut the paper strips. Older children can measure and cut their own strips. You can either perform this activity step-by-step with the class or prepare a model, give directions, and have the project completed independently. Some children may wish to add a whimsical hat, a pipe, a handbag, or some other item to the skeleton. Some may wish to write a poem or short story about it. This can be added to the back of the paper.

This activity is excellent for developing skills in listening and following directions.

Bibliography

Books

Bennett, Jill. *Teeny Tiny*. Boston: Houghton Mifflin, 1989.

Bright, Robert. *Georgie*. New York: Scholastic, 1968.

Brown, Ruth. *A Dark, Dark Tale*. New York: Dial Books, 1981.

Bunting, Eve. *Scary, Scary Halloween*. New York: Scholastic, 1989.

Calhoun, Mary. *Wobble the Witch Cat*. New York: Morrow, 1958.

Devlin, Wende, and Harry Devlin. *Cranberry Halloween*. New York: Aladdin Books, Macmillan, 1990.

Druce, Arden. *Witch, Witch, Come to My Party*. New York: Childs Play, 1992.

Edwards, Pat. *Nobody*. Evanston, Ill.: McDougal, Littell, 1991.

Ehlert, Lois. *Red Leaf, Yellow Leaf*. San Diego: Harcourt Brace Jovanovich, 1991.

Epstein, June. *Leaves*. Cleveland, Ohio: Modern Curriculum Press, 1989.

Hutchins, Pat. *Rosie's Walk*. New York: Scholastic, 1987.

——. *Good-Night, Owl!* New York: Trumpet Club, 1991.

Kalan, Robert. *Jump, Frog, Jump*. New York: Scholastic, 1981.

Krensky, Stephen. *Christopher Columbus*. New York: Random House, 1991.

Kroll, Steven. *The Biggest Pumpkin Ever*. New York: Scholastic, 1984.

Low, Alice. *The Witch Who Was Afraid of Witches*. New York: HarperCollins Children's Books, 1978.

Martin, Bill, Jr. *Brown Bear, Brown Bear*. New York: Henry Holt, 1967.

——. *Polar Bear, Polar Bear*. New York: Henry Holt, 1991.

Martin, Bill, Jr., and John Archambault. *The Ghost Eye Tree*. New York: Scholastic, 1985.

——. *Barn Dance*. New York: Henry Holt, 1986.

——. *Listen to the Rain*. New York: Henry Holt , 1988.

——. *The Magic Pumpkin*. New York: Henry Holt, 1989.

——. *Knots on a Counting Rope*. New York: Trumpet Club, Bantam Doubleday Dell, 1990.

——. *Chicka Chicka Boom Boom*. New York: Scholastic, 1991.

Marzillo, Jean. *In 1492*. New York: Scholastic, 1991.

Nelson, JoAnne. *The Witches' Little Sister*. Cleveland: Modern Curriculum Press, 1989.

Ryan, Cheli D. *Hildilid's Night*. New York: Macmillan, 1971.

Tetherington, Juan. *Pumpkin, Pumpkin*. New York: Scholastic, 1989.

Undry, Janice. *A Tree Is Nice*. Harper Trophy, Harper and Row, 1956.

Whipple, Thomspon Gleiter. *Christopher Columbus*. Nashville, Tenn.: Raintree, 1985.

Williams, Linda. *Little Old Lady Who Was Not Afraid of Anything*. New York: Trumpet Club, 1990.

Williams, Vera. *A Chair for My Mother*. New York: Greenwillow Books, 1982.

———. *Cherries and Cherry Pits*. New York: Greenwillow, 1986.

———. *Music, Music for Everyone*. New York: Greenwillow, 1984.

Ziefect, Harriet. *In a Scary Old House*. New York: Picture Puffins, Penguin, 1989.

Zimmerman, H. Werner. *Henny Penny*. New York: Scholastic, 1989.

Poems

Aldis, Dorothy. "What Am I?" In *Poems of Early Childhood*. New York: Field Enterprises, 1949.

———. "My Brother." In *Time For Poetry,* edited by May Hill Arbuthnot. Chicago: Scott Foresman, 1951.

Farjean, E. "Down, Down." In *The Sound of Poetry*, edited by Mary C. Austin and Queenie B. Mills. Boston: Allyn and Bacon, 1963.

Fisher, Aileen L. "Fall." In *Time for Poetry*, edited by May Hill Arbuthnot. Chicago: Scott Foresman, 1951.

Fyleman, Rose. "The Goblin." In *Time For Poetry*, edited by May Hill Arbuthnot. Chicago: Scott Foresman, 1959.

"Hello Halloween." Racine, Wis.: Copycat Press, 1989.

Lindsay, Vachel. "The Frog." In *Poetry Posters*. Cleveland: Modern Curriculum Press.

Livinston, Myra Cohn. "12 October." In *The Random House Book of Poetry for Children*, edited by Jack Prelutsky. New York: Random House,1983.

"Magic Vine." In *The Big Book of Science Rhymes and Chants*. Monterey, Calif.: Evan-Moor, 1991.

Moncure, Jane B. "Fall Hills." In *In Fall*, by Rochelle Nielsen-Barsuhn, Jane B. Moncure, and E. Hammond. Chicago: Children's Press, 1985.

Neilsen-Barsuhn, Rochelle. "Leaf Dance." In *In Fall*, by Rochelle Nielsen-Barsuhn, Jane B. Moncure, and E. Hammond. Chicago: Children's Press, 1985.

"Old Gus Goblin." Racine, Wis.: Copycat Press 1989.

Prelutsky, Jack "Skeleton Parade." In *It's Halloween*. Pretlutsky, Jack. New York: Scholastic, 1977.

Sendak, Maurice. "October." In *Chicken Soup with Rice*. New York: Scholastic, 1987.

Reference

Baldwin, Lillian. *Music for Young Listeners: The Blue Book, The Crimson Book, The Green Book*. Morristown: Silver Burdette, 1951.

Commire, Anne. *Yesterday's Authors of Books for Children*. Detroit: Gale Research, 1977.

Rudin, Ellen. "Author of the Month: Bill Martin, Jr. and John Auchambault." New York: The Trumpet Club, 1990.

Author's Music

The following is a series of books illustrating and telling famous musical stories:

Fantasia Pictorial. Gakken

Peter and the Wolf

Carnival of the Animals

Invitation to the Dance

Swan Lake

The Sorcerer's Apprentice

Coppélia

Hansel and Gretel

The Nutcracker

William Tell

Moore, Karen. *N O T E*. Stevensville, Michigan: Educational Service, 1973.

3
NOVEMBER

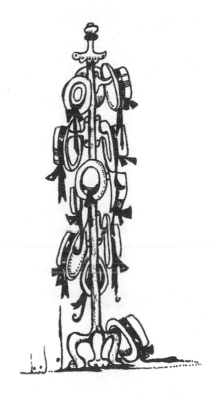

Theme: Madeline Teaches Social Studies

The thematic instruction for this month focuses on map skills, reasons for the Pilgrims' migration to America, and Thanksgiving.

Week 1: Overview

Instructional Book

Madeline by Ludwig Bemelmans

Related Titles

Madeline and the Gypsies by Ludwig Bemelmans (to be read aloud)
Madeline's Rescue by Ludwig Bemelmans (to be read aloud)
Getting to Know the World's Greatest Artists: Mary Cassatt by Mike Venezia
    (to be read aloud)

Poems

"November" by Maurice Sendak
"Maps" by Dorothy Brown Thompson
"Indian Children" by Annette Wynne

Music

An American in Paris by George Gershwin

Objectives

1. **Phonetic skills**
   Begin to understand long a.
   Begin to understand the rule of silent (magic) e.
   Review vowels previously presented.
2. **Structural skills**
   Review the concept of compound words.
   Begin to identify contractions.
   Recognize words that form contractions.
   Review nouns, verbs, and adjectives.
3. **Comprehension**
   Continue to make predictions.
   Review the concept of cause and effect.

Materials

Word cards in the shape of Madeline's hat

World map or globe

Map of Paris

Passport

Pictures of impressionist paintings from sources such as art books and calendars

Brown construction paper

Poetry and Skills Session

DAY 1

"November"

Step 1: As the whole group reads the poem "November," ask the children to identify the words that contain long a.

Step 2: Present the rule for silent e.

Step 3: Ask the children to locate words in which the e affects the sound of the a. Reinforce this skill in small group instruction.

DAY 2

"Indian Children"

Step 1: Read "Indian Children."

Step 2: Discuss the meaning of the poem.

Step 3: Discuss the rhythm and identify rhyming words.

Step 4: Ask the students to identify nouns and verbs in the poem.

Step 5: Introduce the silent e.

Step 6: Ask for examples of words that have an e at the end.

Step 7: Read the poem again for pleasure.

Step 8: Distribute copies of the poem for students to illustrate and include in their poetry notebooks.

DAYS 3 and 4

"Maps"

Maps are an important part of this unit. Spend at least two sessions with this poem, encouraging the children to relate the need for a map when preparing for a trip.

- Ask the children to relate personal experiences with maps. Perhaps they have watched their parents use maps during a trip.

- Review the discussion about the location of France.

- Find Paris on a map of France.

- Read "Maps" to the class. Encourage questions about words that are unfamiliar: *bazaar, ice floes,* and *vagabonds.*

DAY 5

Read from poetry books for enjoyment.

Reading Instruction

DAY 1

Biographical sketch of Ludwig Bemelmans

Mr. Bemelmans was born in Merano, Italy, on April 27, 1898. He did not do well in school because he did not like to have others telling him what to do. His family tried sending him to boarding school, but that was not successful either. He went to live with and work for an uncle who owned several hotels. Mr. Bemelmans was not happy working for his uncle, so in 1914, at the age of 16, he left for the United States with letters of introduction to hotel managers.

He arrived in New York City and found work as a busboy at the Hotel Astor. In World War I, he joined the U.S. Army. He became an American citizen when the war ended. He worked in restaurants until 1924, when he bought the Hapsburg House in New York City. The restaurant was located near publishing houses, and many of his customers were editors and others in the publishing business. He decorated the walls of his restaurant with scenes that reflected his home and the German origin of his cuisine. May Massee, the editor who worked with Robert McCloskey, author of several children's books including *Make Way for Ducklings,* suggested that Mr. Bemelmans write and illustrate a book for children.

His first book was *Hansi,* published in 1934. The proceeds from the sales allowed him to get married and have time to write *Golden Basket,* printed in 1936. It was a Newberry Honor Book and introduced Madeline, a character he named after his wife. These books were based on his experiences in hotels and working with people. His fifth book was *Madeline,* and it was published in 1939. Madeline's bout with appendicitis in the first of the series is based on his own vivid recollections of a road accident in France.

He had trouble getting *Madeline* published because editors felt it was too sophisticated for children. Five years after its completion, Simon & Schuster accepted it for publication, and the book was a tremendous success. In spite of its success, it was 14 years before the next book was published. He won the Caldecott Medal for *Madeline's Rescue* in 1954.

Mr. Bemelmans enjoyed writing and illustrating. His favorite place to write was in the bathtub. He placed his typewriter on a tray that went across the tub. When he died of cancer at age 64 (October 1, 1962), he was working on his sixth book about Madeline (Cech 1983).

Shared Reading

Step 1: Introduce *Madeline* to the class. Have the class discuss the cover and predict the story line of the book.

Step 2: Assess students' knowledge of France and Paris by allowing discussion and the sharing of information. Use a globe or large map to locate France. Also locate the home state of the class. Ask the following questions:

- What direction is our state from France?
- What method of transportation would we use to go to France?
- Based on the location of France on the globe and compared to our state, what kind of climate would they probably have?
- If you were planning a trip to Paris, what would you need to take?

Step 3: Read the story to the class.

Small Group Instruction

Arrange the class in mixed ability groups for this session. Ask the children to look for words in the book that demonstrate various phonetic concepts: long a, e, and i; silent e; compound words; nouns; verbs; and so on. All students will be successful to varying degrees and should be allowed to help each other. The book can then be read aloud as a choral reading.

DAY 2

Biographical Sketch of Ludwig Bemelmans

Shared Reading

Step 1: Present the biography of Ludwig Bemelmans. The children will enjoy hearing about his method of writing. Discuss implications of this method:

- How would the rest of his family feel about his using the bathtub for writing?
- Would this cause any problems?
- What kind of typewriter would he use? (Focus on safety.)
- Could he have used a word processor?

Step 2: Reread the story.

Step 3: Discuss the kind of school Madeline attended. Encourage the children to share information about someone they know who has gone away to school. Discuss the advantages and disadvantages of attending a boarding school.

Small Group Instruction

EL:

Step 1:   Direct the students to choose eight to ten words from the story for further work. Have them dictate several sentences about the story that include these words. The students will add to this story during the next two reading sessions, thus developing their own version of the story. Help them write the beginning of their version during this session.

Step 2:   As the sentences are written on the board, discuss the use of capital letters and periods, and the spelling of some words. The children can help with beginning, ending, and medial sounds. Duplicate these sentences for later use.

TL:

Step 1:   Have the children read the book silently, offering help as needed. Discuss the content of the story as each page or two, depending on the ability of the group, is read. Allow time for discussion of illustrations and the way they reflect the action in the story.

Step 2:   Ask each student to choose one of the pages to read aloud.

AL:

Step 1:   Have the students read the book silently.

Step 2:   Ask them to locate unfamiliar words. The most probable words will be *solemn*, *disaster*, *envy*, and *appendix*.

Step 3:   Help them define each new word. Encourage discussion of these words. Locate the appendix on the body. Model the use of the dictionary to define words.

DAY 3

Shared Reading

Step 1:   Begin an imaginary journey to Paris. Discuss the mode of transportation that will be chosen. Lead a discussion about the choices and the implications of those choices. For example, if the children choose to fly it will be a short journey. If a boat trip is chosen, different preparation may be necessary because of the length of time spent on the ship.

Step 2:   Help the children think about what is needed for travel in a foreign country. They may not be aware that electrical systems are different. A hair dryer from the United States will not work in European countries because of the differences in plugs and current. How do people who travel abroad prepare for this?

Step 3: Discuss money and language problems that can be encountered by international travelers.

Step 4: Following this discussion, give the children 12-by-18-inch construction paper to make a suitcase (they fold it in half crosswise in a hamburger fold, staple the sides, and cut a hole in the top for a handle) and drawing paper to color and cut out into items they feel are essential for a trip abroad.

Small Group Instruction

El:

Step 1: Using the story written in the previous session, have the children read the sentences aloud.

Step 2: Ask comprehension questions about the sentences. Ask various students to read the answers. Focus on the vocabulary the students have selected.

Step 3: Use a drawing of a hat like Madeline's for making word cards. As the children master vocabulary, add a few more words to the list.

Step 4: Have the children write the middle of the story. Record it on the board.

Step 5: Distribute copies of the story written during the previous session, and have the children illustrate them. Collect these papers, which will be used for evaluating comprehension.

Step 6: Duplicate the second part of the story for later use.

TL:

Step 1: Continue guided silent reading. The book should be completed during this session.

Step 2: Ask the children to compare Madeline's school with their own. Are there some similarities? What are the differences?

Step 3: Encourage the children to choose a partner and reread the book independently.

AL: Have other Madeline books available. Ask each child to choose a different book and read it. This silent reading should be done during small group instruction time, with help offered as needed. Encourage the children to continue making note of words that are new.

DAY 4

Shared Reading

For this session, a map of Paris (available through the American Automobile Association and travel agencies) will be needed, as will picture books of France and Paris. These are usually available in the reference section of libraries.

Step 1: Review the location of France, then Paris.

Step 2: Discuss the fact that Paris is in a country outside the United States so anyone who goes there will need a passport. If possible have an example of a passport to show the class. Help the children understand the need for and use of passports.

Step 3: Using the map of Paris, enlarge the central section so the students can locate the Eiffel Tower, the Louvre, the Arc de Triomphe, etc.

Step 4: Give each child a copy of the map of Paris, and begin a sightseeing tour. First stop is the Eiffel Tower. Give the children information about the tower (its height, age, etc.). Locate it on the enlarged map of Paris.

Step 5: Find the Champs Elysees and the Arc de Triomphe. Discuss the sidewalk cafes along the street and their importance in the social life of people who live in Paris.

Small Group Instruction

EL:

Step 1: Ask the children to share their illustrations from the first session.

Step 2: Read the two pages of the story the children have composed.

Step 3: Continue with the dictation process and have the children create an ending to their story. Write this on the board; duplicate it later.

Step 4: Have the children read their stories silently or with a partner, including the final segment from the board. Help them evaluate what has been written by asking questions that will draw attention to details about Madeline:

- Could they have used more describing words?
- Did the sentence say what they intended?

Step 5: Select one of the sentences. Add several adjectives to help students understand how sentences can become more "colorful" through the use of appropriate words. Ask them to illustrate the second section.

TL:

Step 1: Define and give examples of adjectives. Encourage the children to add examples. Ask the students to look through the story and identify some of the adjectives.

Step 2: Make a list of adjectives that describe Madeline. Take time to encourage the students to go beyond simple words like *nice* and *bad*.

Step 3: Ask students to think of adjectives that describe themselves. Using some of these adjectives, have the children write two or three sentences comparing themselves with Madeline. Have these illustrated and display them in the room.

AL: Ask this group to compare *Madeline* to the other Bemelmans book they read. Begin by discussing the setting. Give each child a sheet of paper and ask that they draw two large, overlapping circles to make a Venn diagram. Label one circle *Madeline* and the other circle with the name of the other book they read. As each question is asked, write the word in the appropriate place. If both stories took place in Paris, write "Paris" in the overlapping section. (*Madeline in London,* for example, will have "Paris" in *Madeline* and "London" in the other circle.)

Ask whether all of the stories took place in Paris and whether the same characters appeared in each story. At the end of the comparison, the children will be able to see the similarities of the stories.

DAY 5

Getting to Know the World's Greatest Artists: Mary Cassatt

Shared Reading

Step 1: Locate the Louvre on the map of Paris.

Step 2: Discuss the contents of this famous museum. Tell the class a little about the kind of art they might find there. The *Mona Lisa* is in this museum, and many children are familiar with this painting by Leonardo da Vinci.

Step 3: Talk a little about Impressionism, which had its beginning in Paris.

Step 4: Read *Getting to Know the World's Greatest Artists: Mary Cassatt* to the class. Encourage them to comment on how the pictures are different from photographs or other works of art. Libraries contain many books that will enrich this discussion.

Small Group Instruction

EL: Distribute the third segment of the story. Put the pages together in a book. All children should select a name for their book and write their own name as author and illustrator on the cover. Encourage the children to decide whether their artistic style is realistic or Impressionistic and to give reasons to support their evaluations. Children should design covers for their books.

If desired, they can write a dedication and the name of their school as the publishing company. This will be determined by the awareness of the students. If author, illustrator, and publisher have been discussed each time a book has been introduced, the children will want to include these in their own copies. It makes them more REAL.

Allow time for the "authors" to enjoy and share their books.

TL:

- Review the definition of adjectives, offer several examples, and encourage the children to add their ideas.

- Lead a discussion about the instances in which Madeline did not obey the rules. Invite the children to share experiences about a time they broke a rule. Ask them to write two sentences about something they did that was against the rules. Let them decide whether or not to share these with their classmates.

AL: Encourage this group to discuss the range of plots Mr. Bemelmans used. Call attention to the plot of *Madeline* and the fact that this is based on his experience in France following an automobile accident. Spend some time speculating about the source of the other plots.

Ask each child to suggest an idea for a new story. This may be done by writing or drawing a series of numbered pictures and allowing time to explain each plot.

Independent Activities

Materials

Construction paper for get-well cards

Passport

Extension Activities

- Draw pictures of Mr. Bemelmans sitting in his bathtub, writing the Madeline stories.

- Make a passport by folding a piece of typing paper in fourths. On the front, write "Passport for (child's name)." (Fold reproducible on p. 3-11)
  On inside pages, duplicate the following:

Name	About myself:
Age	Stamp of Approval
Birthdate	Places I have visited:
Birth place	1. through 8.
Picture (Draw self-portrait in this space.)	

On the back cover, draw a United States flag and design an official seal.

PASSPORT FOR

Name _____

Age _____

Birthdate _____

Birthplace _____

Picture

About myself _____

_____

_____

_____

Stamp of approval

Places I have visited

1. _____

2. _____

3. _____

4. _____

5. _____

6. _____

7. _____

8. _____

• Make literature squares (see diagram that follows) with French words on the outside and the English words on the inside. Illustrate the words.

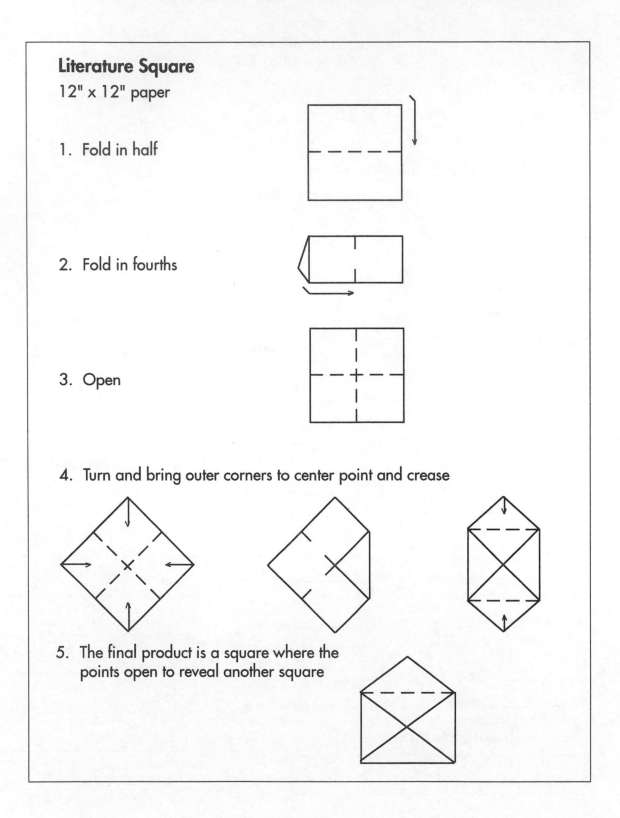

Literature Square

12" x 12" paper

1. Fold in half

2. Fold in fourths

3. Open

4. Turn and bring outer corners to center point and crease

5. The final product is a square where the points open to reveal another square

- Choose one of the Madeline books and write a literature report identifying main characters, setting, problem, and solution.

Small Group and Center Activities

- Begin a scrapbook of Paris (see diagram on p. 108). The names of the sights can be written by the students or duplicated on a sheet of paper, cut apart, and pasted at the bottom of each page. The students then draw pictures of them.

- Madeline is in the hospital and is feeling very sad. Get-well cards always cheer patients, so have the class make cards for her.

- Rewrite the story of *Madeline,* with each student contributing an idea. Have them write their sentences at the bottom of 12-by-18-inch paper. They are to illustrate the pages and then combine them into a class big book.

Math

This lesson deals with the concept of twelve.

- List items that are packaged in boxes of twelve.

- Make a booklet of story problems that relate to Madeline. Fold a sheet of 9-by-11-inch paper and write one problem on each page.

   If _____ little girls go away, ten little girls are left. Write the subtraction sentence.
   If _____ little girls go away, two little girls are left. Write the subtraction sentence.
   If three little girls go away _____ little girls are left. Write the subtraction sentence.
   If six little girls go away _____ little girls are left. Write the subtraction sentence.

Social Studies

Map-reading skills are incorporated into each session. Use a large map of the world or a large globe to show the locations of the home state and France. Help the children establish points of reference on the globe: North Pole, South Pole, equator, and Atlantic and Pacific Oceans. Ask questions about directions from their home state in relation to these reference points on the globe.

SCRAPBOOK

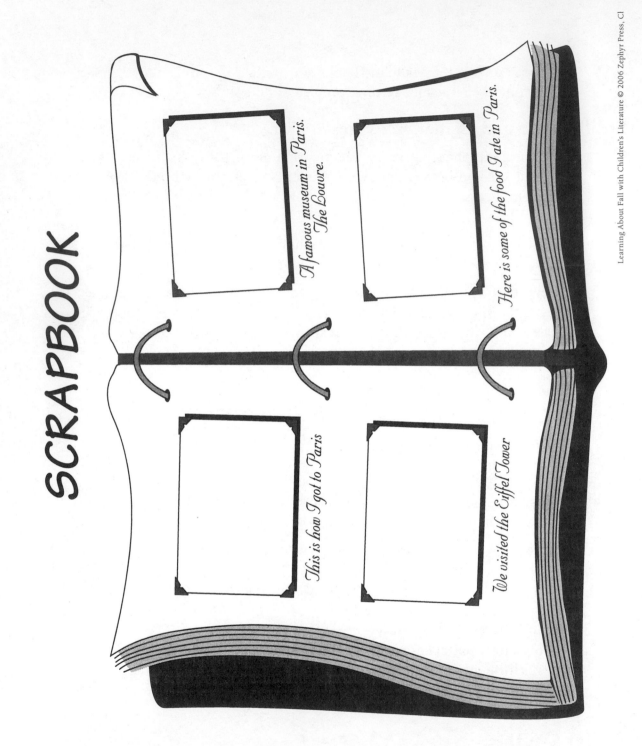

A famous museum in Paris.
The Louvre.

Here is some of the food I ate in Paris.

This is how I got to Paris

We visited the Eiffel Tower

Foreign Language

Teach the children to say "hello" in French.

The children should have some knowledge of the points of interest in Paris and how the names sound. If French is not a part of the curriculum, ask a parent or teacher volunteer to assist. It is important for children to be aware that there are differences in language and culture. If French is not taught, the purpose is to introduce the students to the sounds of a different language.

Music

An American in Paris by George Gershwin offers a musical experience that will help students visualize the traffic of Paris as well as the hustle and bustle of the city. Play it several times during this week with no comment, thus giving the children the opportunity to become familiar with it.

Art

Continue discussing artistic style so the children will be able to differentiate between Impressionism and realism. A general understanding of these two styles is all that is desired. If an art teacher, parent, or community volunteer is available, ask that person to assist. Local art museums often have volunteers who will come to the school to provide classroom support.

Week 2: Overview

Instructional Books

> *Madeline and the Bad Hat* by Ludwig Bemelmans
> *Bonjour Mr. Satie* by Tomie dePaola
> *Jessica* by Kevin Henkes

Related Titles

> *Linnea in Monet's Garden* by Christina Björk

Poems

> "Riddle" by Christina Rossetti
> "Wild Geese" by Jane Belk Moncure

Objectives

1. **Phonetic skills**
   Begin to recognize "sight" family words.
   Begin to understand long and short i.
   Begin to understand words ending with y.
   Recognize rhyming words.

2. **Comprehension**
   Review the concept of main idea.
   Begin to find supporting facts.

3. **Social studies**
   Continue to develop map skills.

Materials

Word cards in the shape of Pepito's hat

Paper for individual books

Poetry and Skills Session

DAY 1

"Riddle"

Step 1: Introduce the poem to the students and read it together.
Step 2: Identify the rhyming words.
Step 3: Direct the children's attention to "sight." By changing the beginning sound, make a list of the new words in this "family." Continue adding to the list as the children work in small groups.

DAY 2

"Riddle"

Step 1: Identify the words that contain long i and those that contain short i. Circle the long-vowel words with washable green marker and the short-vowel words with red.
Step 2: As the poem is read, have the children clap on short i words.
Step 3: Read again, clapping on long i words.

DAY 3

"Wild Geese"

Step 1: Introduce the poem by asking the students what they know about wild geese. Encourage them to conclude that geese migrate in the fall and that this is a sign of the change in the season.

Step 2: Read the poem several times to help children become familiar with the content.

Step 3: Identify the words that contain long i and those that contain short i.

Step 4: Discuss the sound of y at the end of the words in the poem. Present the concept that y is the chameleon of the alphabet, sometimes acting as a vowel, sometimes as a consonant.

DAY 4

"Wild Geese"

Migration of animals is one sign of winter. Let this poem motivate a discussion of other signs of winter.

DAY 5

Read poetry books for fun and fluency.

Reading Instruction

DAY 1

Shared Reading

Step 1: Read one of the other Madeline titles to the class.

Step 2: Discuss the similarities of the stories.

Step 3: Draw a Venn diagram. Label one circle *Madeline* and the other with the title of the other book.

Step 4: Compare facts, landmarks, characters, and action by using this tool.

DAYS 1 – 5

Small Group Instruction

EL: Use the same procedure you used the previous week. Select vocabulary for the story and write a page each day, completing a second "book" for this group. In using words from the story, the pupils are also learning basic vocabulary. Duplicate what is written each day so the children can read and illustrate it during the next session.

Encourage these students to read their books to a partner. If possible, arrange for them to go to a kindergarten class and read the completed books.

TL: Read the second title in the same way *Madeline* was read during the previous week

AL: During this week, read stories about other children. Ask the school librarian to help locate books that have a child's name in the title. This allows a variety of reading levels to be included so that everyone has appropriate books. These books should be shared during the week.

Have the children do simple book reports that include the following information:

- Title

- Author and illustrator

- Where the story takes place (setting)

- General time of story

- Characters in the story

- A line or two about the story and a recommendation to others in the group about the story (Was it enjoyable? Was the title a good indicator of the story?)

DAYS 2 – 5

Shared Reading

During these discussions, ask the entire group questions based on Bloom's Taxonomy (1956) about the Madeline books.

- Knowledge

  Name the animals mentioned in the Madeline stories.
  Tell the naughty things that Madeline did.
  Name all the places in Paris that you can find in the Madeline stories.

- Comprehension

  Why did Madeline go to a boarding school?
  How is a boarding school different from your school?
  How are the Madeline stories alike?
  Describe the things needed for the care of a horse.

- Application

  How would the "house all covered with vines" need to change to take care of a horse?
  Who would care for the animal when the school closes for vacations?
  How could the horse get exercise and food in Paris?

- Analysis

  What are some of the problems of keeping animals in a boarding school?
  Could the gypsies really have taken Madeline and Pepito?
  What part of this story could have been true and what part fiction?

- Synthesis

  Madeline keeps tearing her clothes. What kind of clothes should the little girl wear?
  The children are tired of breaking bread at each meal. Make up a new menu for them.
  It is the birthday of one of the other little girls. The parents want to give her something all the children can play with at the same time. What could they give her?

- Evaluation

  Madeline did many naughty things in the stories. Make a list, from the most insignificant to the most serious.
  Pepito also did some very naughty things. Choose the worst and tell how he should be punished.

These questions should be discussed in a whole-group setting. The children can be asked to write one or two sentences about a question that is particularly interesting to them. Children who are more able can work with the emergent readers and produce their results in pairs. Assignments should follow extensive discussion, encouraging all children to share information and ideas. Display the results of this assignment in a prominent place. Allow time for the children to share their work with the class.

Independent Activities

Materials

Large paper bags: grocery bags or slightly smaller ones

Construction paper: yellow, pink, blue, white, and red

Patterns for Madeline doll, or dolls cut free-hand by the children

Sentences duplicated for comprehension activity

Watercolor paints and paper

Extension Activities

- Have each student make a large Madeline doll. They will use a large grocery bag for the base, pink paper for the face, hands, and legs, blue paper for the dress, and yellow paper for the hat. Then they are to write a story, which can be attached to the flat "bottom" of the bag and the face and hat placed over it.

- Duplicate the following sentences on paper. Using large manila paper folded into fourths, have the students cut the sentences apart, place them in sequence, and illustrate this paper.

  Madeline could frighten Miss Clavel.
  In the night, Miss Clavel said "Something is not right."
  There were twelve little girls in two straight lines.
  The smallest was Madeline.
  The little girls tiptoe in with solemn faces.

- Plan a French luncheon. This in a good opportunity to ask someone in the school or community to help as a resource person. Serve the luncheon at a sidewalk cafe that the children "construct" in the room.

Small Group and Center Activities

- Make a picture dictionary of landmarks in Paris. Have the students draw pictures of important points in Paris: the Arc de Triomphe, the Eiffel Tower, a sidewalk cafe, etc. The students can write the label under the picture. Aternatively, labels can be written for them, to be copied. The students then paste them under the appropriate pictures. Common French words can be included, along with the English translations.

- Ask students to paint a picture in either an impressionistic or realistic style.

- Write a story that begins, "I would be a/an (impressionist or realist) artist because . . . "

114

Science and Math

Step 1: List the animals mentioned in the books about Madeline.

Step 2: Sequence them from largest to smallest.

Step 3: Sequence them from the easiest to the most difficult to care for in a city.

Step 4: Working in small groups, have children research the needs of these animals.

Social Studies

- Give each child a map of the world. Using this map, locate the places discussed in the unit: the home state and approximate location of their city, the Atlantic Ocean, France, Paris, Holland, England, and London.

- Discuss the following:

  Methods of travel to France
  Direction from children's home
  How Madeline traveled to London
  How a horse could be moved from London to Paris

Foreign Language

Introduce common French words. These words can be placed in a "French Dictionary" and illustrated. It is also appropriate for the words to be duplicated for the children rather than requiring them to be written. Include a word each day of the two-week unit.

Music

George Gershwin was an American who composed beautiful music during the early twentieth century. Among his best known works are *Rhapsody in Blue* and *An American in Paris.*

Gershwin visited Paris for the first time in the summer of 1923 and was immediately enchanted with the city. He felt that it was a city you would write about and wanted to be the one who did the writing. However, it was not until 1928 that he made this dream come true.

An American in Paris opens with the image of an American walking down the Champs Elysees. The American hears the sounds of the city, passes a cafe, crosses the river, and sits at an outdoor cafe on the Left Bank. A blues theme is introduced here, suggesting that the American has become homesick. The switch to a Charleston theme suggests that the traveler has discarded this feeling and is prepared to enjoy the city life of Paris (Taylor 1960).

As the first part of the musical work is played, help the children identify the sounds of the traffic. Correlate this with pictures of the Champs Elysees and the mad traffic on this boulevard.

In other sessions, help the children relate other knowledge of Paris to the music. Encourage them to use their imaginations to "see" their own pictures.

Art

Continue the discussion and comparison of realism to impressionism. Calendars are a good source of inexpensive pictures that can be taken apart and used in the classroom. Numerous books in the library can help the children begin to develop an awareness of artistic style. Discuss the feelings the colors evoke and the use of primary, pastel, warm, and cool colors. Encourage the children to verbalize their reactions to the various combinations of colors.

Week 3: Overview

Instructional Books

The Pilgrims' First Thanksgiving by Ann McGovern
Best Thanksgiving Book by Pat Whitehead

Related Titles

The Thanksgiving Story by Alice Dalgliesh (to be read aloud)
How Many Days to America? A Thanksgiving Story by Eve Bunting (to be read aloud)

Poems

"Were You Afraid?" by Beryl Frank
"Books" by Eileen Burkarad Norris
"Day Is Done" by Lee Bennett Hopkins

Objectives

1. **Phonetic skills**
Review and relearn phonetic skills previously introduced.

2. **Structural skills**
   Strengthen knowledge of nouns, verbs, and adjectives.
3. **Alphabetizing skills**
   Strengthen alphabetizing skills.

Materials

Word cards in the shape of a turkey, pilgrim's hat, or other symbol of Thanksgiving

Poetry and Skills Session

DAY 1

"Were You Afraid?"

Step 1: Introduce the theme of the next two weeks: Pilgrims. Begin by asking the children to list all they know about the Pilgrims. Write these statements on a large chart. Allow plenty of time for discussion and comparison of facts. At this time, do not react in any way to ideas that are not accurate. The broader the range of "facts," the more meaningful the two-week study will be.

Step 2: Read the poem "Were You Afraid?"

Step 3: Allow time for the children to imagine what it would have been like to be a Pilgrim and make this journey.

DAY 2

Step 1: Review the discussion and the preconceptions stated during the previous lesson.

Step 2: Reread the poem.

Step 3: Ask the children to identify the adjectives in this poem.

Step 4: Read some of the lines without the adjectives. Encourage the children to notice how these words add "color" to the poem.

Step 5: Read the poem again, with the students clapping each time an adjective appears.

Step 6: Choose a line that has several adjectives, and help the children locate the nouns being described. Ask for other words that would describe the noun.

Step 7: Distribute copies of the poem for your students to illustrate and include in their poetry notebooks.

DAY 3

"Books"

Step 1: Introduce the poem through a discussion of how we know about the Pilgrims. Help children to verbalize that information about the past is "history" and can be found in books.

Step 2: Read the poem "Books." Relate it to the discussion.

Step 3: Identify nouns in the poem.

Step 4: Distribute copies of the poem for your students to illustrate and include in their poetry notebooks.

DAY 4

"Day Is Done"

Step 1: Today is a day for a little comic relief. Ask for examples of Thanksgiving Day and what happens in the homes of the children. Encourage the sharing of experiences, particularly some of the difficult moments.

Step 2: Introduce the poem "Day Is Done." Read it several times for appreciation of content, rhythm, and rhyme.

Step 3: Ask whether the students are ever asked to help clean up the dishes. Allow time for appreciation of the less glamorous side of Thanksgiving.

Step 4: Distribute copies of the poem for your students to illustrate and include in their poetry notebooks.

DAY 5

Today is for individual and small-group sharing of favorite poems. It is appropriate for you to request poems to be read by the group.

Reading Instruction

Shared Reading

During the shared reading sessions, be alert to students who need extra help with particular skills. Group the students who need reinforcement or reteaching.

Each day during the two-week study of Pilgrims, read a book or continuing story about the topic. Suggestions have been made, but any book on the subject may be used.

Select appropriate words as the target vocabulary. The students can share in this process, or you can make the selections. Much of the vocabulary will be appropriate for illustration and can be compiled into a dictionary reinforcing alphabetizing skills presented earlier. Over a period of approximately two weeks, working with two or three letters each day, the students will each be able to make a complete, illustrated dictionary of Thanksgiving words. Several words can be chosen for each letter, allowing the children to individualize their books.

Small Group Instruction

DAY 1

EL: Group children who need help with vowels or other identified skills. Play "Space Talk," as follows:

Have children select a planet they wish to visit. In order to visit, they need to speak the language. Have them take turns asking a question of the alien who lives on the planet. Example: "What do you eat?" Write a response on the board. Have a child sound it out. This response is a nonsense word but will include the skill that needs reinforcement. "Pamp" reinforces a short a. "Mape" reinforces the silent e rule. It may help if you write several of these nonsense words down before the session.

The children become very involved in this game, and you can encourage them to think of unusual questions. You must be ready to "translate" the answers. For example, in response to "What do you eat?" you may explain that "pamp" means rocks dipped in chocolate. As the game is played, the children can suggest meanings for the words. This encourages creativity on everyone's part. Children love this game, and they do not realize how it strengthens the use of decoding skills. The game is appropriate for all levels of ability; there are no wrong answers.

TL:

Step 1: Introduce *Best Thanksgiving Book*. Begin with questions that help the students make predictions about the story.

Step 2: Discuss the illustrations. Are they realistic or impressionistic? Encourage the use of the vocabulary presented in the art sessions.

Step 3: Allow time for the children to leaf through the book and talk about the alphabetical format. Relate this book to those the students are making. Encourage them to see that these pictures have sentences at the bottom of the page that include the word. If some students wish to do this in their own books, it should be encouraged.

Step 4: Read several of the pages, making note of words that are difficult. At the conclusion of the group, write these words on the board and discuss the clues for decoding them.

AL:

Step 1: Introduce *The Pilgrims' First Thanksgiving*. This book has six sections and should be read as a "chapter" book. Depending on the ability of the students, read a page or a section silently and follow with comprehension questions. (Some of this is appropriate for whole-class participation.)

Step 2: Focus on questions about why a certain action was taken.

Step 3: To help the children truly understand the discomfort on the ship, ask them to lie still on the floor for five to ten minutes. Then ask them to imagine sleeping there for three months.

Step 4: Discuss the difficulty of making decisions about possessions to include.

Step 5: Encourage the students to talk about how the Pilgrims felt leaving family that they would probably never see again.

DAYS 2, 3, and 4

Best Thanksgiving Book

EL:

Step 1: Introduce the book to the group. Read it aloud together.

Step 2: Identify words to use for vocabulary development. Write them on turkey-shaped cards cut from brown construction paper. Encourage the children to use the target words in sentences that retell the story of the first Thanksgiving. These sentences will become the basis for a Thanksgiving big book.

Step 3: Write the sentences on large paper. Let the children illustrate them. Continue the writing of the book through the week.

Step 4: Review the vocabulary together.

TL:

Step 1: Ask each child to choose a favorite letter and read that page aloud. Give immediate help with difficult words.

Step 2: Suggest that this group make a big book of their own Thanksgiving words. Let the children work in pairs so they can support each other. Each pair is to choose a letter and a word that begins with that letter. They should write the letter, a word beginning with that letter, and a sentence containing the word on a 12-by-18-inch sheet of paper.

Step 3: Have the children illustrate the work and, depending upon the number of pairs involved, pace themselves so that the book can be completed by the end of the week.

AL: Continue with the next section of *The Pilgrims' First Thanksgiving*. Again avoid factual questions, encouraging the students to think about why actions were taken and what the implications would be. Take time to help them identify the factors important to the Pilgrims when they selected the site for their new home: water, safety, and land that would be cleared and easy to cultivate.

DAY 5

EL and TL: Each group now shares its book with classmates. Arrange for the groups to take their books to another class, perhaps a kindergarten, and read to them.

AL: This group may need the following week to complete the discussion of *The Pilgrims' First Thanksgiving*. Allow ample time to read the book and discuss the material.

At the end of the book, ask each child to write a short story about why he or she would or would not have liked to be a pilgrim. If the children have difficulty doing this independently, they can work with partners. They might even work as a whole group to produce a big book.

Independent Activities

Materials

Shapes for tracing to make compound-word game

Spices to glue on hand-shaped turkey

Chart with American Indian symbols

Brown paper (grocery bags are good)

Pasta that has been colored and dried

Large paper for mural

Extension Activities

- Thanksgiving is a good motivator for working on compound words. The children can trace around pictures of an assortment of things found on a table: knife, cup, sugar bowl, or other simple-to-draw items. They are to cut these pictures in half and write part of a compound word on each part. They can exchange their puzzles with friends. Example:

    cook   book

- Encourage the children to add to a list of compound words as they read and discuss the material on Pilgrims and Thanksgiving.

- Tape a large piece of butcher paper to the wall. Let the children draw a large mural of the first Thanksgiving.

- Draw pictures of the first Thanksgiving, and write a story as though the writer were present.

- Write and illustrate the menu for the first Thanksgiving.

- Corn was an important part of the diet of Pilgrims and American Indians. Ask the children to make a list of the ways corn is used today. They might bring in favorite corn recipes and compile a class corn cookbook.

Small Group and Center Activities

- To illustrate the smells of Thanksgiving, either bring an assortment of spices to class or ask children to bring some samples in small containers. Provide brown construction paper. Have each child trace the shape of his or her hand on the paper and cut out the shape. The thumb is the head of a turkey. Glue is placed over the end of each paper finger, and each is dipped in a different spice.

- Make a large chart of the American Indian symbols (see p. 123 for examples). Using the symbols, write messages on pieces of paper and have the children decode them. They can create their own messages.

- Make an animal skin by tracing the shape of an animal on a flattened brown paper bag. Decorate the paper with American Indian symbols. Wad and smooth the paper repeatedly until it becomes soft. It feels like suede if this is done long enough.

- Color dried pasta and string to make necklaces.

Science

- Discuss the problems with food on the trip to the "New World." Discuss the importance of keeping food from spoiling.

- Experiment with drying some food. Apples and grapes work well for this experiment.

Picture Language Dictionary*

Chief	Indian Camp	Journey	Desert	Snow
Rain	Deer Tracks	Deer	Dead Deer	Mountains
River	No Food	Hungry	Eat	Death
Woman	Days & Nights	Fish	Forest	Plenty Food
Deep Snow	Many	Friendship	Child	Wisdom

* Adapted from Dunn, Dorothy, *American Indian Paintings,* Albuquerque, N.M.: University of New Mexico Press, 1968; and Amon, Aline, *Talking Hands,* Garden City, N.Y.: Doubleday, 1968.

- Water was a problem for the Pilgrims. Allow a container of water to stand (covered) overnight, and let the children taste the difference between it and fresh water. If possible, allow some water to stand in a wooden container and note the flavor of wood. Relate this to conditions on the Mayflower.

- Mix salt in water. Have the children rub some on the backs of their hands and allow it to dry. Discuss what it would feel like to bathe in salt water.

Math

- The Mayflower was about 70 feet long, and there were 102 people on it. Measure this area on the playground, and invite enough children to join the class so there are that number on the "ship."

- Estimate how much water is consumed in a day by each student. Provide paper cups for each child; have them measure and record what they drink for one day. Working as a group, calculate what the entire class drank. How much water would be needed for a week?

- Make a list of the various uses for water. Which of these would probably not be allowed on a ship, where water is limited?

Music

Play recordings of music that evokes images of being on a ship or on the ocean. As the music plays, have the children close their eyes and imagine being on a ship, rocking to make it more believable. Say "Pretend you are on the Mayflower. You have been here for many days. There is no place to play because the ship is small and there are many people. You look out and can see only water. Every day you eat the same dried food and drink stale water. The ship never stops rocking."

Do this several times, adding different ideas as the children become more familiar with the process. Elicit suggestions from them. This activity will help them appreciate how difficult it was for the Pilgrims to come to America.

Week 4: Overview

Because this is Thanksgiving week, plans for three days are included. No instructional books are included for the week. The students will use the writing activities for reading purposes.

Related Title

Books available locally

Poem

"On Thanksgiving Day" by Rochelle Nielsen-Barsuhn

Materials

Ingredients for food to be prepared for feast

Chart paper for writing recipes

Poetry and Skills Session

DAY 1

"On Thanksgiving Day"

Read the poem together. Discuss similarities and differences between the holiday as presented in the poem and the observances in the homes of the students. Allow plenty of time for sharing. You should also share some personal experiences.

DAY 2

Have the class write a name poem, using the letters in *Thanksgiving*.

Reading Instruction

Shared Reading

Step 1: Discuss what the children have learned about the reasons the Pilgrims came to America. Highlight the difficulties they faced and the problems they shared. Consider the help they received from Indians and how they tried to show their gratitude.

Step 2: Suggest that the class plan a Thanksgiving feast to be shared with another class or with parents. Guide the planning session. Help them plan a menu that will be authentic and simple enough to prepare in the classroom. Cornbread, butter, fruit salad, and popcorn are simple foods that can be cooked by the children. The feast does not have to take the place of a meal but can be served in the afternoon. Use this week to plan and prepare the food.

Step 3: After the food for the class feast has been prepared, have the children write recipes that they think the Pilgrims might have used in preparing the first Thanksgiving feast. How many pounds of cornmeal would be needed for the bread? What would be the baking procedure? What would be the baking time? Record these recipes on large chart paper to be displayed during the feast.

Step 4: The children can also present their Thanksgiving books as a short program to parents or students from another class.

Science and Math

Materials

Whole milk and a container of whipping cream

Small jar with a lid that screws on tightly

Colored popcorn

Fruit cut into pieces

Lemon juice

- Write on the board the recipes for the food to be prepared. Use the math time to increase the quantities for the number of people to be served.

- Combine a half-pint of cream with a quart of milk. Let the mixture stand until the cream rises to the top. Help the students understand that this is where cream comes from.

- Skim the whipping cream from the milk. Explain that if you shake this cream, butter will form. Ask the children to estimate how much butter will be produced by the pint of cream. Record the estimates. Place the cream in a jar with a tight lid, and let the children take turns shaking it until the butter forms. Compare the results with the estimates. Have the children calculate how much cream would be needed to make a pound of butter. After the butter has formed, allow each of the children to taste the buttermilk.

- Each child can bring a half-cup of cut fruit for a friendship salad to be served at the feast. Calculate how much this will make, and estimate whether it will be enough to share.

- Ask why some fruits turn dark after they have been cut. How can this be prevented? Does it change the taste of the fruit? Does lemon juice keep the fruit from turning dark? Why?

- Discuss the items used to make cornbread and the function of each in the recipe. Observe the change in looks, taste, quantity, and texture before and after baking. Allow the children to measure, mix, and prepare the cornbread for baking.

- Estimate the amount of popcorn needed to give each person a share. Discuss the change in popcorn during the heating process. What causes the corn to expand?

- Is colored corn colored when it pops? Why not? Why do some kernels remain unpopped? Speculate on who popped the first corn. How could it have happened?

Foreign Language

Teach the children words of welcome in the target language. Greet the guests with these words.

Music

The music played during the previous week can become the background music for the feast.

Art

- Make invitations for the guests.
- Prepare place mats, Pilgrim hats, Pilgrim collars, Indian headbands, and vests for the feast. Vests can be made from grocery bags, as follows: Cut up the seam. Cut circles for the arms and neck. Cut a fringe along the bottom and decorate with Indian symbols.

Bibliography

Books

Amon, Aline. *Talking Hands*. Garden City, N.Y.: Doubleday, 1968.

Bemelmans, Ludwig. *Madeline*. New York: Viking Penguin, 1939, 1954. Reprint, Scholastic.

———. *Madeline's Rescue*. New York: Viking Penguin, 1951. Reprint, Scholastic.

———. *Madeline and the Bad Hat*. New York: Puffin Books, Penguin Books, 1956. Reprint, Scholastic.

———. *Madeline and the Gypsies*. New York Puffin Books, Penguin Books, 1959. Reprint, Scholastic.

———. *Madeline in London*. New York: Puffin Books, Penguin Books, 1961.

Björk, Christina. *Linnea in Monet's Garden*.

Bunting, Eve. *How Many Days to America? A Thanksgiving Story*. New York: Trumpet Club, 1992.

Dalgliesh, Alice. *The Thanksgiving Story*. New York: Scholastic, 1990.

dePaola, Tomie. *Bonjour, Mr. Satie*. New York: Scholastic, 1992.

Dunn, Dorothy. *American Indian Paintings*. Albuquerque, N.M.: University of New Mexico Press, 1968.

Henkes, Kevin. *Jessica*. New York: Scholastic, 1989.

McCully, Emily Arnold. *Mirette on the High Wire*. New York: Scholastic, 1993.

McGovern, Ann. *The Pilgrims' First Thanksgiving*. New York: Scholastic, 1973.

Venezia, Mike. *Getting to Know the World's Greatest Artists: Mary Cassatt*. Chicago: Childrens Press, 1990.

Whitehead, Pat. *Best Thanksgiving Book*. Mahwah, New Jersey: Troll Associates, 1985.

Poems

Frank, Beryl. "Were You Afraid?" In *Poetry Place Anthology*, edited by Rosemary Alexander. New York: Scholastic, 1983.

Hopkins, Lee B. "Day is Done." In *Poetry Place Anthology*, edited by Rosemary Alexander. New York: Scholastic, 1983.

Moncure, Jane B. "Wild Geese." In *In Fall*, by Rochelle Nielsen-Barsuhn, Jane B. Moncure, and E. Hammond. Chicago: Childrens Press, 1985.

Nielsen-Barsuhn, Rochelle. "On Thanksgiving Day." *In In Fall*, by Rochelle Nielsen-Barsuhn, Jane B. Moncure, and E. Hammond. Chicago: Children's Press, 1985.

Norris, Eileen B. "Books." In *Poetry Place Anthology*, edited by Rosemary Alexander. New York: Scholastic, 1983.

Rossetti, Christina. "Riddle." In *The Sound of Poetry*, edited by Mary C. Austin and Queenie B. Mills. Boston: Allyn and Bacon, 1963.

Sendak, Maurice. "November." In *Chicken Soup with Rice*. New York: Scholastic, 1987.

Thompson, Dorothy B. "Maps." In *The Random House Book of Poetry for Children*, edited by Jack Prelutsky. New York: Random House, 1983.

Wynne, Annette. "Indian Children." In *For Days and Days*. New York: J. B. Lippincott, 1919.

References

Bloom, Benjamin S. *Taxonomy of Educational Objectives: The Classification of Educational Goals—Handbook I, Cognitive Domain.* New York: David McKay, 1956.

Cech, J., editor. *Dictionary of Literary Biographies.* Detroit: Gale Research, 1983.

Taylor, Deems. "Notes." *An American in Paris.* New York: Radio Corporation of America, 1960.

SCOPE AND SEQUENCE FOR
Learning About Winter with Children's Literature

DECEMBER

Author: Frank Asch

English Skills
  Phonetic skills
    Vowel digraphs
    Vowel with r
  Structural analysis
    Root words

Science Skills
  Seasons
    Animals in winter
      Bears
        Migration and hibernation

Social Studies Skills
  Holiday customs in
    Israel
    France
    Italy
    Mexico
    Germany
    England
    Russia
    United States

Music Skills
  The Nutcracker

JANUARY

Author: Frank Asch

English Skills
  Phonetic Skills
    Consonant blends
      Beginning
      End
  Structural Analysis
    Synonyms
    Homonyms
    Antonyms
    Plural and possessive nouns
    Apostrophe
  Comprehension
    Comparing
    Contrasting
    Book reports

Science Skills
  Birds
    Characteristics
    Identification and parts
    Adaptation for winter
  Winter
    Signs of
    Adaptation of animals

Math Skills
  Calendar
  New year
  Graphing of weather
  Counting by 2

Social Studies Skills
  Compare weather, seasons of
    two hemispheres

FEBRUARY

Author: Rita Gellman

English Skills
- Phonetic skills
  - Vowel diphthongs
  - Endings -er, -est
- Structural analysis
  - Pronouns
  - Verb tense
  - Alphabetizing to second letter
- Comprehension
  - Categorizing
  - Main idea
  - Topic sentences
  - Supporting facts

Science Skills
- Human body
  - Bones
  - Lungs and breathing
  - Heart and blood
  - Brain and nerves
  - Stomach and Digestion
  - Skin
- Health
  - Nutrition
    - Food groups

Social Studies Skills
- History of pasta
- Abraham Lincoln
- George Washington

Math Skills
- Calendar
- Patterning
- Categories

SCOPE AND SEQUENCE FOR
Learning About Spring with Children's Literature

MARCH

Author: Mercer Mayer

English Skills
Structural analysis
Commas
Comprehension
Drawing conclusions
Summarizing
Similes
Parts of a Book
Science Skills
Dinosaurs
Characteristics
Earth during dinosaur age
Our changing Earth
Math Skills
Measuring
Weights

APRIL

Author: Leo Leoni

English Skills
April and May are used to
reinforce and reteach phonetic,
structural analysis, and
comprehension skills
Science Skills
Mammals
Whales
Rabbits
Characteristics of mammals and fish
Sharks
Health
Teeth
Math Skills
Multiplication
Double digit addition and
subtraction
Social Studies Skills
Map skills

MAY

Author: Robert McClosky

Science Skills
Deserts
The Earth's surface
Social Studies Skills
Maps and globes
Location of deserts and oceans

NOTES

NOTES

NOTES

NOTES

NOTES

NOTES